WARRIOR • 152

ROYAL NAVAL AIR SERVICE PILOT 1914–18

MARK BARBER

ILLUSTRATED BY ADAM HOOK

Series editor Marcus Cowper

First published in Great Britain in 2010 by Osprey Publishing
Midland House, West Way, Botley, Oxford OX2 0PH, UK
44-02 23rd St, Suite 219, Long Island City, NY 11101, USA
E-mail: info@ospreypublishing.com

A CIP catalogue record for this book is available from the British Library

ISBN: 978 1 84603 949 2

E-book ISBN: 978 1 84603 950 8

Editorial by Ilios Publishing Ltd, Oxford, UK (www.iliospublishing.com)
Page layout by: Mark Holt
Index by Sandra Shotter
Typeset in Sabon and Myriad Pro
Originated by PDQ Media, Suffolk
Printed in China through Worldprint Ltd

10 11 12 13 14 10 9 8 7 6 5 4 3 2 1

AUTHOR'S NOTE

The views and opinions expressed in this text are the author's alone and do
not represent the views of the Ministry of Defence.

EDITOR'S NOTE

All photographs in this book are taken from the Fleet Air Arm Museum.

ARTIST'S NOTE

Readers may care to note that the original paintings from which the colour
plates in this book were prepared are available for private sale.
All reproduction copyright whatsoever is retained by the Publishers.
All enquiries should be addressed to:

Scorpio Gallery
PO Box 475
Hailsham
East Sussex
BN27 2SL
UK

The Publishers regret that they can enter into no correspondence upon
this matter.

THE WOODLAND TRUST

Osprey Publishing are supporting the Woodland Trust, the UK's leading
woodland conservation charity, by funding the dedication of trees.

CONTENTS

ROYAL NAVAL AIR SERVICE PILOT 1914–18

INTRODUCTION: THE ORIGINS OF NAVAL AVIATION IN BRITAIN

With the great number of years it takes to develop a modern military aircraft, it is sometimes difficult to appreciate the vast level of technological advancement in aviation that was brought about by World War I. The year 1903 saw the world's first powered, heavier-than-air flight, with the Wright brothers' 12hp Flyer I, capable of reaching speeds of 30mph (48km/h), remaining airborne for 12 seconds on its maiden flight at Kitty Hawk. By the time the Royal Naval Air Service (RNAS) was absorbed into the newly formed Royal Air Force (RAF) on 1 April 1918, the naval variant of the Sopwith Camel single-seat scout was capable of launching from a warship and climbing to an altitude of 15,000ft (4,570m) in 25 minutes, where, with a maximum speed of 117mph (188km/h) provided from its 150hp engine, it could engage enemy aircraft with its two machine guns.

These quantum leaps in aviation were, however, a slow process, which even the most farsighted individuals within the Admiralty could not have foreseen. Although in 1903 many within the ranks of the Admiralty passed aviation off as having no military potential, there were some who saw a maritime application for flight. Samuel Franklin Cody, an American aircraft designer, first approached the Admiralty in February 1903 with his design for a manned kite which he claimed, when towed from a warship, could reach heights of 1,200ft (365m) to carry out reconnaissance, signalling and gunfire direction. The kites could also be used to carry aerials, thus massively increasing the range of communications.

Five weeks later, trials of these kites were carried out in Portsmouth, achieving impressive results. The subsequent report stated that the use of kites for communications could be relied upon, but in anything other than ideal conditions the kite was too unsafe for manned aviation. Cody's price was, however, too high for the Admiralty who promptly purchased four kites from another designer. Although further development of kites continued, the Admiralty's real interest at this point lay with airships. Airships could keep pace with surface ships and had an endurance and load-carrying capacity far greater than contemporary heavier-than-air craft. Rear Admiral Lambton had campaigned for interest in military ballooning, and a committee was set up in June 1903. The committee submitted a demand for a navigable balloon, capable of reaching altitudes of 5,000ft (1,524m) and remaining aloft for three days with a crew of three. This specification was, in effect, the first call for pilots in the Royal Navy.

The first lighter-than-air aircraft to be purchased by the Royal Navy was the Willow non-rigid airship, which flew in September 1905, but only to a height of 120ft (37m). The development of the non-rigid airship continued up to and throughout World War I, but the next stage of the evolution of airships was the semi-rigid airship; this design incorporated a keel fitted on the underside of the gas bag under which was slung the gondola and power plant. The final stage in development was the rigid airship, which housed its gas bags within a frame covered by a fabric envelope. The rigid airships were easier to handle and moor, and the more stable design resulted in larger aircraft with greater capabilities. Although the British Army had also showed an interest in airships, the Admiralty took control of all lighter-than-air aircraft in November 1913. Naval airships were used throughout the war for gunnery spotting and patrolling.

Whilst there had been some interest generated in aviation within the Admiralty, it was in the field of heavier-than-air flight that the least amount of interest lay. This was somewhat ironic considering that even within the four years of World War I, this area would witness not only the greatest technological advances, but also the greatest capability in terms of supporting the Army and the Royal Navy. The Wright brothers, together with several other individuals, continued to advance the development of the heavier-than-air aircraft in the early years of the 20th century. By 1905, the Wright brothers were producing aircraft with a range of 25 miles (40km), and two years later they approached the Admiralty with a view to selling their designs. Unfortunately, the Wright brothers were turned down by the Royal Navy, although they did receive a military contract with the US Army the next year. Lord Tweedmouth, the First Lord of the Admiralty, wrote to the Wright brothers on 7 March 1907, stating: 'I have consulted my expert advisors with regard to your suggestion as to the employment of Aeroplanes, and I regret to have to tell you, after careful consideration of my Board, that the Admiralty are of the opinion that they would not be of any practical use to the Naval Service.'

Fortunately, the foresighted individuals within the Admiralty soon began to take more of a keen interest in aviation and in July 1908 a recommendation was made to appoint a Naval Air Assistant to their Lordships. On 21 June 1910, Lieutenant G. C. Colmore became the first qualified pilot in the Royal Navy, paying for his own training to earn Royal Aero Club Certificate Number 15. In 1911 the Admiralty called for officers to volunteer to become the first pilots trained within the service. Of approximately 200 volunteers, three naval officers and one officer of the Royal Marine Light Infantry (RMLI) were selected on 1 March: Royal Navy Lieutenants R. Gregory, C. R. Samson, A. M. Longmore and RMLI Lieutenant E. L. Gerrard.

Gerrard later recorded many of his memories of the early days of naval aviation in an essay entitled 'Early Days of Flying'. He writes: 'I never had any confidence in Airships, what I knew of meteorology convinced me that their life was ephemeral, and when the Navy called for volunteers for aeroplanes, my name was easily the first in.' He goes on to describe his three fellow *ab initios*, beginning with Samson, the senior officer to be selected for pilot training: 'He came to us from the Persian Gulf where he had been hunting Pirates, doubtless his fierce pointed beard helped to inspire terror in the wrong-doer. There was a rumour he got sunstroke in the Gulf.' Gerrard recalls Gregory as a particularly superstitious pilot, who once switched off his engine immediately after take-off,

Charles Rumney Samson was one of the original four officers selected to be the first naval pilots. He is pictured here as a wing commander during the Dardanelles campaign, with his Nieuport Scout of No.3 Wing. His aircraft has a Lewis gun positioned to fire directly up through the centre section of the upper wing.

landed and promptly walked to the aerodrome accommodation hut: 'I followed to enquire the trouble, he was looking worried, with a very large whiskey and soda in his hand, he said: "My God, I nearly left the ground and it is Friday!"' Finally, Gerrard describes Longmore and Cockburn, their instructor: 'Longmore says he was selected because he was regarded as expendable, and would leave no widow to claim his pension! I think his good looks and tactful bonhomie must have helped. Cockburn … had studied with Henri Farman in France, he took infinite care with us and none of us so much as broke a wire up to the time of taking our "tickets", though afterwards we had some adventures.'

The four were trained by the Royal Aero Club (RAeC) at Eastchurch on the Isle of Sheppey. Samson and Longmore were the first to qualify, gaining certificates 71 and 72 respectively on 25 April. Gregory and Gerrard earned certificates 75 and 76 on 2 May.

Whilst the Royal Navy had been taking steps to further aviation, so too had the Army. In 1912, the Royal Flying Corps (RFC) was officially formed, its origins lying in the Air Battalion of the Royal Engineers, which itself was a development of the Royal Engineers' Balloon Section, formed in 1890. The proposal submitted in April 1912 called for the RFC to be divided into both a Military and a Naval Wing – the Naval Wing would initially be equipped with four biplanes and four monoplanes of various designs, and also six sets of floats to convert the aircraft into seaplanes, or 'hydro-aeroplanes' to use the contemporary terminology. Hand in hand with this proposal was the formation of a joint Army and Navy aviation school at Upavon – this, however, had been delayed by the Royal Navy's own establishment at Eastchurch, which now had six training aircraft. The Eastchurch school was clearly producing results – in January 1912, Lieutenant Samson, one of the first four student pilots, became the first pilot to launch from a warship, taking to the air in a Short S38 biplane from a wooden deck attached to the forecastle of HMS *Africa*, which lay at anchor in Sheerness Harbour at the time. The honour of the first ever flight from a vessel underway also fell to the Naval Wing on May 9, when a Short S38 launched from HMS *Hibernia* in Weymouth Bay.

An aerial view of RNAS Eastchurch in winter 1914. It was the very first Royal Naval Air Station, and also home of a Royal Aero Club strip and a Short Brothers factory. After transferring charge to the RAF, the station was closed in 1946.

The pioneering Samson was given command of the Naval Wing, which by the summer of 1913 consisted of 31 aircraft, including ten seaplanes that were now regularly launching from a wooden deck fitted to the cruiser HMS *Hermes*. Samson also became the first pilot to experiment with dropping bombs from a heavier-than-air aircraft, and under his command the first transmission of a wireless signal was carried out from a Short seaplane. The Admiralty was, however, not satisfied with the state of affairs regarding aviation; the RFC was, after all, an Army unit and the Admiralty was keen to have its own aviation as an independent naval practice. This was made evident not only by the continued support of the Eastchurch training school, which had trained over 100 naval pilots by the beginning of 1914, but also by the formation of the Air Department of the Admiralty in 1912, under the command of Captain M. F. Sueter, who had supervised the construction of the airship *Mayfly*. Sueter's hands were tied in many ways by the RFC, but his grasp of the potential of military aviation was ahead of its time, as shown by his address to the Committee of Imperial Defence, when he explained that 'war in the air, for the supremacy of the air, by armed aeroplanes against each other is likely'.

Naval Airship No.1, the *Mayfly*, photographed after its launch from Cavendish Dock, Barrow-in-Furness in 1911. The *Mayfly* broke in two during a test flight on 24 September of the same year.

Under Sueter's administration, the RNAS was officially formed on 1 July 1914. In addition to continuing its role with heavier-than-air aircraft, the RNAS also adopted responsibility for all British military airship operations. In August A. M. Longmore, another of the original four Eastchurch pilots and now a squadron commander, set another aviation first when he dropped a 14in. torpedo from his Short Folder seaplane. This trial had been personally requested by the First Lord of the Admiralty, Winston Churchill, who, influenced by the now Commodore Sueter, had been a staunch advocate of naval aviation for some time. The

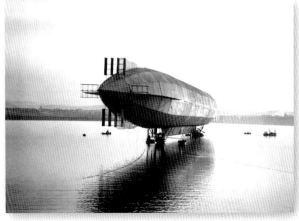

achievements of Sueter and the air and ground crews of the RNAS came not a moment too soon – seven days after the first torpedo drop, on 4 August 1914, Britain declared war on Germany in response to the German violation of Belgian neutrality, and the RNAS was plunged into World War I. British naval aviation had, in the face of much adversity, progressed a great deal since the Wright brothers' first flight only one decade previously, a fact recognized by Churchill and highlighted in his 1913 speech to the Lord Mayor's Banquet in London: 'Our hearts should go out tonight to those brilliant officers, Commander Samson and his band of brilliant pioneers, to whose endeavours, to whose enterprise, to whose devotion it is due that in an incredibly short space of time our naval aeroplane service has been raised to that primacy from which it must never be cast down.'

CHRONOLOGY

1903	Samuel Franklin Cody approaches the Admiralty with offers to produce kites for shipborne reconnaissance. Cody's offer sparks the first real interest in aviation within the Royal Navy and a committee for military ballooning is established in June. In December the Wright brothers make history with the world's first powered heavier-than-air flight in Kitty Hawk, North Carolina.
1905	The Willow non-rigid airship is the first aircraft purchased by the Royal Navy, carrying out its first flight in September. The Wright brothers approach the Royal Navy with offers to build aircraft.
1907	The Admiralty formally rejects the Wright brothers' offer of aircraft, being of the opinion that heavier-than-air aircraft have no practical military use.
1908	The post of Naval Air Assistant is created.
1910	On 21 June, Lt. G. C. Colmore becomes the first qualified pilot in the Royal Navy, after funding his own training.
1911	The Admiralty issues a signal, asking for volunteers for flying training. Lieutenants R. Gregory, C. R. Samson, A. M. Longmore and E. L. Gerrard are selected to be the first pilots trained within the Royal Navy. The Royal Navy's first rigid airship, His Majesty's Airship No.1 – the *Mayfly* – is destroyed during her airborne trials in September.
1912	Lieutenant C. R. Samson becomes the first pilot in the world to launch from a warship in January. On 13 April the Royal Flying Corps is formed. Royal Navy pilots are employed within the Naval Wing of the RFC. On 9 May the Naval Wing achieves another world first by launching an aircraft from a warship making way. The Air Department of the Admiralty is formed.
1913	The Admiralty takes control of all lighter-than-air aircraft in the British military. Royal Navy aircraft carry out the first

ever wireless transmission and bomb drops from heavier-than-air aircraft.

1914   On 1 July the Royal Naval Air Service is formed. On 28 July Lt. Longmore becomes the first pilot ever to drop a torpedo from an aircraft. On 4 August Britain declares war on Germany. On Christmas Day, seven RNAS seaplanes are launched against targets in the vicinity of Cuxhaven, Germany.

1915   Flight Sub-Lieutenant R. A. J. Warneford destroys Zeppelin LZ37 in aerial combat on 7 June, earning the RNAS's first Victoria Cross. The second is earned on 19 November by Richard Bell-Davies, who lands behind enemy lines in the vicinity of enemy troops to rescue a downed comrade. August marks the unofficial beginning of the 'Fokker Scourge' on the Western Front. On 12 August Flight Commander C. H. K. Edmonds becomes the first pilot ever to sink an enemy ship by an air-launched torpedo, destroying a Turkish merchantman in the Gulf of Xeros.

1916   Between May and July, Raymond Collishaw's 'Black Flight' of 10 Naval Squadron scores 87 confirmed kills. Flight Lieutenant F. J. Rutland pilots the only aircraft present during the battle of Jutland, flying reconnaissance duties in a Short Type 184.

1917   The Sopwith Camel enters service with the RNAS in June. On 2 August Squadron Commander E. H. Dunning becomes the first pilot to land on a moving ship, recovering a Sopwith Pup to the deck of HMS *Furious*. He is tragically killed five days later during an attempt to repeat the feat.

1918   On 1 April the RNAS and RFC are dissolved, being merged to create the RAF. At the time of its dissolution, the RNAS employs over 55,000 officers and ratings, operating over 3,000 aircraft and over 100 air stations.

RECRUITMENT AND TRAINING

Recruitment for the new branch of the Royal Navy was not an easy task to formalize, as military aviation had only existed in Britain for two years by the outbreak of the war. As the first signal sent out by the Admiralty had called for officers to volunteer for special duties, the task of piloting aircraft remained predominantly with officers throughout the war. Thus, by the time hostilities began in earnest, the RNAS set about recruiting officers solely with the intention of transforming them into pilots.

Before the war, entry into the Royal Navy as an officer was an accomplishment in its own right. Richard Bell-Davies was a boy at public school in 1901 who sat the naval examination straight from school, at the age of 15. 'There was an ancient custom in the Navy,' Bell-Davies wrote, 'whereby each captain on being appointed to his first command was allowed to nominate one boy to sit for the examination... My uncle... sent him

[Captain Baker RN of the cruiser HMS *Blake*] a letter and I received the nomination.'

The examination process lasted for four days, after which 65 boys were selected from the 300 who sat the exam. Bell-Davies was one of these 65. Those who were successful then began their training as officer cadets at Dartmouth. The purpose-built college was not completed until 1905; prior to this, officer cadets lived onboard either HMS *Hindustan* or HMS *Britannia*, two obsolete hulks moored in the river Dart.

The syllabus itself, designed to educate officers in all branches of the Royal Navy, revolved heavily around seamanship; courses were conducted in operating craft of various sizes, beginning with skiffs in the river Dart and progressing onto large craft navigating around the coastline of Devon and Cornwall. Mathematics also played a very large part in syllabus training and, together with team sports, contributed a greater part of the practical skills and teamwork that would play a large role in the lives of the naval officers who passed out. The cadets would spend four terms of instruction at Dartmouth, each term lasting some three months. With breaks taken between each term, cadets were normally 17 years of age when they passed out as midshipmen.

Once the war began, the process by which potential officers were interviewed and selected was a far cry from the formal process of the Admiralty Interview Board, which came much later. One hopeful, T. D. Hallam, who in October 1914 was a private in a machine-gun battery, sent a cable to the Admiralty and applied to transfer across as a naval pilot. Despite his having a good deal of pre-war experience as a flying-boat pilot in Canada, the Admiralty rejected Hallam on the grounds that 'Colonials made indifferent officers' and that the RNAS had more pilots than it would ever need. Undeterred, Hallam sent in a second application and attacked the interview in a completely different way. In his first interview, Hallam had arrived in his private's uniform and with details of his flying experience; the second time around, he wore a well-tailored civilian suit and carried letters of introduction from people whom he considered to be 'important'. He was immediately offered a commission as a sub-lieutenant in the RNAS, illustrating the unfortunate prejudice and snobbery that were well established in the Admiralty at the time.

As well as sitting an interview, prospective pilots were also subject to a medical examination to ascertain their suitability for aviation. The standards of the medical exam were variable, with less stringent requirements in evidence later on in the war. Charles Bartlett applied for a commission in the RNAS immediately after the outbreak of hostilities, but was rejected due to a heart defect. Bartlett preserved nonetheless and reapplied later on, being accepted as a pilot in 1915 even though he was again subject to a medical examination.

Once selected, the officer training carried out by prospective naval pilots did in no way

Edwin Harris Dunning, here a flight lieutenant, poses for a photograph shortly after being awarded his Distinguished Service Cross for 'Exceptionally good work as a seaplane flyer'. He wears his 'monkey jacket' over the more formal winged collar shirt.

resemble the long, thorough process undertaken by pre-war Dartmouth cadets; by 1916, the only training that separated a civilian from a commission in the RNAS was a week-long course in drill and traditions of the Royal Navy. Another system within which it was possible to fly with the Royal Navy was that of the Short Service Commission (SSC); if successful after the medical examination, applicants were commissioned as probationary sub-lieutenants in the Royal Naval Reserve (RNR) and given a £40 uniform allowance before being sent to flying training. If successful in achieving their brevet, pilots would then be able to claim back the money spent in flying training, something normally in the region of £75. This system bypassed any general naval training whatsoever, leaving RNR officers to attend flying training with no knowledge of military etiquette and procedure.

Flying tuition itself took place at one of several airfields across the UK, but the fundaments of what was taught remained fairly constant. The academic, formalized flying-training syllabus that is used internationally today did not properly evolve until the end of the war, although there was still a programme of sorts for *ab initio* pilots to progress through to obtain their ticket. Flight Lieutenant E. L. Ford recalled in his post-war account *Learning to fly during the Great War* that:

> To qualify, one had to carry out quite a programme consisting of take-offs, landings, left and right hand level circuits, a climb to minimum height (or higher) with a barograph in a sealed box slung around one's neck, execute good figure eights, and finally volplane or glide in with engine dead and hand held well away from the switch then make a smooth landing and come to a standstill within thirty yards of official Royal Aero Club observers who were on the ground watching one's flight throughout.

Ford was one of many naval officers who learnt to fly at the Grahame White Flying School at Hendon. Many students were taught to fly in Bristol

An *ab initio* pilot climbs into an Avro trainer for his first flight. This experience flight was 'for free'; after this taster, every flight would be assessed and the pilot would be constantly graded and evaluated on his performance.

Boxkites, a simple biplane with a tandem seating arrangement with both pilots' seats effectively secured to the centre of the wing and no cockpit to speak of. Only one instrument existed in the Boxkite – a drip-feed oil pulsator which, if dripping steadily, indicated that the oil feed to the engine was satisfactory. Aircraft designed by the Wright brothers were also used for tuition. These aircraft were fitted with a length of chord attached to one of the struts in front of the pilot; if this chord flew out to the left or right, it was an indication that the pilot was flying out of balance, or 'sideslipping'. Flying in such a primitive machine with students with little or no experience required very exacting meteorological conditions. Ford writes:

> Atmospheric conditions at the aerodrome, were ascertained by holding aloft – believe me – a silk handkerchief; if it remained limp or fairly so, we flew – if it flew, we didn't... We were taught to fly and judge our speed by capital 'F' Feel and capital 'S' Sound – a sense of balance and the noise made by the air whistling through wires and around struts. Never, we were told, NEVER rely on instruments; a sensitive seat and delicately tuned ear were much more reliable!

This practice is in complete opposition to modern piloting principles.

Starting the aircraft itself was a team effort, as aircraft were not equipped with starter motors. The pilot would open the throttle just enough to allow a little of the fuel/air mixture through to the engine, whilst a member of the ground crew would stand by the propeller and physically fling it until the engine burst into life. One student pilot, F. Silwood, remembered being so excited by his first solo flight that he could not wait for one of his ground crew to start his propeller, so he ran around to carry out the task himself. Unfortunately he had left the throttle fully open, and as soon as the engine started it powered up fully, tearing across the airfield away from him as he ran after it. The aircraft took off alone, climbed to 50ft (15m) and then nosed over to plough into the ground.

A maintainer turns the propeller of a Sopwith Camel to help the pilot start. Aircraft of the period did not have starter motors, and so this potentially hazardous job fell to the ground crews.

Ground crew guard the wings of a speeding Avro 504. During take-off and landing runs, larger, less-stable aircraft would require runners on the wings until enough lift was generated to self stabilize.

It was not uncommon for student pilots to fly their first 'solo' after a mere hour's dual instruction, and qualifying to wear the coveted brevet or 'wings' would typically be achieved in around six hours of flying, only one of which would be flown solo. As aircraft became increasingly complex throughout the war, so too did flying training, and some student pilots took up to ten hours of flying to achieve their first solo by the latter stages of the war. However, flying solo and earning 'wings' was only the beginning – in the early months of the war, the entire pilot's course at the Central Flying School, which was a mixed establishment catering for both Army and Navy pilots, lasted for some three months. Pilots progressed onto steadily more complex and less forgiving aircraft as their abilities developed.

Interspersed amongst the flying was an intense course of lectures on subjects such as the theory of flight (a subject still very much in its infancy), Morse code, airframes and engines. The last of these subjects proved to be one of the most important, as the embryonic aero engines that powered early military aircraft were notoriously temperamental, and full engine failures leading to forced landings away from the aerodrome were a regular occurrence. Once employed as a front-line combat aviator, the skills required to land without power and then repair an engine behind enemy lines before taking to the sky again proved invaluable to a number of pilots. As military aviation was yet to prove itself at the beginning of the war, the demand to send significant numbers of pilots to the front line was not excessive, so there was ample time to train pilots to an acceptable standard. As the war progressed and the service provided by military aviators became more essential, growing numbers of pilots were needed at front-line squadrons, resulting in inevitable cuts in the training programme in order to facilitate these numbers. These came to a head towards the end of the war, particularly during 'Bloody April' of 1917, where the average life expectancy of a new pilot on the Western Front was two weeks. Consequently, more pilots were needed to fill gaps and training became shorter and shorter, with some pilots reaching the front line with less than ten hours of total flying experience, perhaps only half of this on their actual front-line aircraft type.

For the majority of the war, student pilots would very rarely fly with instructors once they had achieved their first solo. It was only in 1918, after the successes of Major Robert Smith-Barry of the RFC, that the RNAS adopted new instructional techniques. These revolved around sitting the student pilot in the front seat of the aircraft with the full set of controls, and having the more experienced instructor in the more awkward rear seat, with less visibility. Smith-Barry's techniques also included revising the syllabus, insisting that student pilots still required a good deal of dual instruction following their first solo, so that advanced techniques such as steep turns and spin recovery could be taught properly. Following successful completion of spin recoveries with an instructor, students would then repeat the exercise solo – rather than the older technique of experimenting with spinning alone and with no experience, often with fatal results.

Another important change in the last years of the war was the recognition that higher-performance aircraft required a different training syllabus; as a result, pilots who showed certain skills were streamed to fly the more demanding single-seat scouts, and consequently were instructed in faster, more agile training aircraft, whereas those bound for the slower bombers and reconnaissance aircraft were instructed in more docile trainers. Air-to-air combat in particular was given the respect it was due, with new pilots arriving at front-line squadrons being given 'on the job training' in mock dogfights with their flight and squadron commanders before being allowed on patrol. Schools of Aerial Fighting were established in England where experienced combat pilots would be pulled away from the front line to teach dogfighting to student pilots. Primitive gun cameras were used to safely teach air-to-air combat, and embryonic night-flying techniques were also developed, with pilots taking off and landing from strips illuminated with flaming oil barrels. The barrels were laid out to form an 'L' shape so that the short arm of the L could be used as a reference point for pilots taking off and landing, with pilots having to 'rely on balance' immediately following take-off to keep the aircraft level until their night vision was restored and they could pick out a horizon, as instrument lighting was still yet to be developed. Bomber pilots too were given better training, with techniques developed so that bombs could be dropped in differing winds from heights up to 2,500ft (762m). A target would be chalked out in the centre of a range, with dummy bombs being dropped and their position marked by an observer on the ground to aid the pilot in correcting his aim. By 1918, freshly qualified pilots were hitting the front line with a vastly

A   GOING SOLO

A student pilot takes to the air for his first solo flight, flying an Avro 504K at RNAS Cranwell. The Admiralty requisitioned 2,500 acres (1,011 hectares) of land from the Earl of Bristol in November 1915, and the RNAS Training Establishment at Cranwell was commissioned on 1 April 1916. The first solo flight for any pilot is the first important landmark of a career in aviation. The circuit consists of a take-off, level off, turn to fly downwind parallel to the runway, and then a final turn and landing. The circuit is designed not only to establish a formal traffic pattern in the proximity of the airfield, but also to teach accurate flying. After several successful circuits under dual instruction, the student pilot lands to drop off his instructor before taking off again to complete one circuit alone. The instructor watches from the ground along with the student's coursemates. After a successful landing, the student will celebrate in customary naval style by buying a round of drinks for his coursemates.

The Avro 504K was one of the most successful training aircraft of World War I, combining docile handling characteristics with the dual-control layout still used in modern training aircraft, although single-seat combat variants of the 504 were used in several theatres of the war.

A skid-equipped Sopwith Pup lies on top of HMS *Furious'* torpedo tubes after a less-than-successful landing.

superior training package to their compatriots from the beginning of the war only four years previously, with established training syllabi in place that founded the principles of pilot training still used today.

Another vital weapon in the arsenal of the RNAS was airships; the recruitment and training of crews for these was completely separate. The RNAS entered the war with only a handful of airships, but the Admiralty had, by this time, seen the benefits of what airships could provide in terms of reconnaissance, and was happy to fund the extension of the airship arm. Thomas Elmhurst, then a midshipman on HMS *Indomitable*, recalled a signal being sent to all battleships and battle cruisers in the Grand Fleet asking each captain to recommend one officer aged between 18 and 20 years of age for 'special service'. Officers recommended were to possess sound navigational skills and be able to

The pilot and crew of Submarine Scout Zero 37, at RNAS Milton in Pembroke. The blimp's Lewis gun is visible near the nose; it could also carry up to 250lbs (113kg) of bombs.

take charge of a small crew. The rumour flying around wardrooms was that volunteers were required to take command of motor boats in the canals of Flanders to assist the British Expeditionary Force (BEF), but those officers who volunteered soon discovered the real reasoning.

The first volunteers, upon reporting to the Admiralty, were taken directly to see Lord Fisher, the First Sea Lord, who told them that they had been selected to fly airships to counter the U-boat menace, also adding that they would in all probability be dead within the year, but might earn a Victoria Cross in the process. Volunteers were told that they had 48 hours to consider the duties of an airship pilot, and that they would be paid an extra ten shillings a day.

Flying training itself began on simple balloons to teach pilots the fundamentals of lighter-than-air aviation. Students were given instruction on how to rig and inflate a balloon, conducting several flights with an instructor before their first solo flight. Controlling a balloon was a relatively simple affair – the balloon travelled in a direction dictated by the wind, and would climb to an altitude governed by the point at which the gases within the bag stopped expanding. The balloon would then more often than not begin a gentle descent, which would be countered by releasing some ballast from the basket by throwing a few handfuls of sand over the side from the attached sandbags. Landing was a slightly more complicated procedure, with pilots having to judge their groundspeed against their rate of descent to land in the most suitable area they could find. Whilst this form of aviation was still in its infancy and inherently dangerous, the rate of casualties amongst pilots learning to fly balloons, or 'balloonatics' as they called themselves, was notably lower than their heavier-than-air brethren.

After demonstrating the requisite skills on balloons, student pilots then progressed to powered airships. The small Submarine Scout airships consisted of the fuselage of a BE2C aircraft hung underneath a gas bag. The pilot's instrument panel consisted of an altimeter, an airspeed indicator and pressure gauges to show the atmospheric pressure and the pressure of the gas bag above

Ground crews struggle to bring in a Submarine Scout Zero at RNAS Polegate. In 1918 a blimp of this type set a record by staying airborne for 50 hours and 55 minutes.

them, which was governed by a simple pump. The controls consisted of a rudder bar, which acted in the sense of a boat's tiller rather than that found on a conventional aircraft, with left-foot pressure sending the airship to the right, and an elevator wheel positioned directly in front of the pilot. The pilot also controlled the flow of air into the forward and aft segments of the balloon, and had strings to release water ballast. Finally, two gas valves could also be operated to regulate the pressure within the gas bag.

Landing proved to be much more of an ordeal in an airship; pilots would attempt to approach their landing area as slowly as possible, typically at a speed of 10–20mph (16–32km/h). Ropes were lowered from the airship which then snaked along the ground, and ground crews would then throw themselves onto the ropes and be dragged across the ground at speeds of up to 20mph (32km/h) until the airship came to a halt, after which it would descend to land. It was important for ground crews to allow the ropes to contact the ground first, as otherwise the ground crews themselves would act as earthing points for the airship as soon as they grabbed the ropes, causing them to suffer electric shocks. Once competent with their airship, pilots would be awarded their wings and sent on to operational duties.

EQUIPMENT: FLYING CLOTHING AND UNIFORM

Aside from the specialist clothing required to carry out the duties of an aviator, the Royal Naval pilot wore the standard kit issue provided to or purchased by officers of any branch in the Royal Navy. The uniforms themselves were dependent not only upon the occasion, but also on the climate in which the officer was serving. For routine, day-to-day duties, RNAS pilots wore 'Daily Working Rig'; this consisted of trousers and a double-breasted 'monkey jacket', furnished with two rows of four gold buttons bearing the Royal Navy's fouled anchor motif, and gold lace around the cuffs to denote rank, the top row of this

DAILY WORKING RIG, 1917

This pilot wears the standard blue officer's working dress. The double-breasted jacket, or 'monkey jacket', has eight gilt buttons with an eagle motif to designate that this officer is a direct entrant into the RNAS. This officer holds the rank of squadron commander, denoted by three rings of gold lace on the cuff, the middle of which is narrower than the upper and lower. This rank is the equivalent to that of lieutenant-commander in the surface fleet, although a squadron commander with less than eight years' seniority would wear only two gold laces, accompanied by two stars above the executive curl of the upper lace. Above the executive curl, the pilot wears a gilt eagle on each cuff to denote him as a pilot. Prior to June 1917 both pilots and observers wore the same flying badge (**8**), but on 22 June a flying badge for observers was formalized, which was a winged letter 'O'. The pilot wears a soft-collared white shirt (allowed instead of the winged collar from June 1916 onwards) and black tie. Also worn are trousers with black patent-leather shoes. From June 1916, lighter grey trousers were permitted as an alternative for individuals working in hotter climates or on airfields. Finally, the pilot wears a peaked cap, the badge of which consists of two sprays of laurel leaves around the gilt eagle of the RNAS. Pilots who transferred from the regular Royal Navy kept their fouled anchor on both their cap and buttons. A white cap cover was worn over the dark cap between May and September.

Further details of the various RNAS officer rank insignia are also shown:
1. Wing captain
2. Wing commander
3. Squadron commander
4. Squadron commander (less than eight years' seniority)
5. Flight commander
6. Flight lieutenant
7. Flight sub-lieutenant

lace coiled into an 'executive curl'. Medal ribbons were worn above the left breast pocket. The actual material of the jacket and trousers varied in quality, as officers were expected to source their own uniforms privately from a tailor, as opposed to the issue clothing that was provided to ratings.

Officers of the RNAS also wore a flying badge – a metal eagle – placed above the executive curl on their left sleeve. This ruling was changed in April 1916 to ensure that only officer aircrew (i.e. pilots and observers only) wore the flying badge. It was specifically placed on the sleeve to make it as discreet as possible, as individuals within the Admiralty felt that steps needed to be taken to avoid glamorizing the role of the aviator within the Navy. Two months later the ruling was clarified further, with an observers' badge consisting of a letter 'O' with wings being introduced leaving the eagle motif exclusively for the use of pilots, now to be worn on both sleeves. The origins of the flying badge itself date back to 1913, when Captain Murray Sueter, the head of the Admiralty's Air Department, submitted a brooch that his wife had found in Paris as a design for the Naval Wing's flying badge – the eagle design of the brooch was accepted. Rating pilots wore the same eagle on their right sleeve, above a three-spoke wheel, with both badges finished in red.

In addition to the flying badge, a gold six-pointed star was worn on the cuff above the eagle to denote flight commanders, as both flight commanders and flight lieutenants wore the two gold rank stripes of a general-service lieutenant. To further complicate matters, squadron commanders with less than eight years' seniority also wore only two stripes, but wore two stars vertically above their flying badge. Wing captains who held the rank of commander in the general service also wore this star, above three gold stripes.

The jacket was worn over a white shirt with soft collar and black tie, together with shoes or boots of black leather. Officers also wore peaked caps with a patent-leather peak and black mohair band, upon which was sewn the cap badge. The badge consisted of two clusters of laurel leaves in gold gilt, in between which was a silver fouled anchor. Atop this was a gold gilt crown, the king's crown and queen's crown being noticeably different depending upon who the reigning monarch was. For officers who joined the service directly into the RNAS, rather than transferring across from the general service, the silver fouled anchor was removed and replaced with a silver eagle. The eagle also replaced the anchor on the jacket buttons for direct entry pilots. The cap itself was black, although during summer months and when serving in warmer climes a white cap cover was worn over the top of the black cap and tucked into the band.

This uniform varied very little throughout the course of the war, though, as of June 1916, officers were allowed to wear more practical trousers of grey flannel for airfield duties. Another practice that was developed out of the necessity for a more practical uniform was the RNAS Overseas Service Dress for officers. Throughout 1914 officers stationed on the Western Front wore the standard Daily Working Rig identical to those officers stationed in the UK; as of 1915, the local unofficial practice was to wear khaki uniforms based heavily on the Army Service Dress. This consisted of a khaki single-breasted jacket with shoulder straps worn with khaki trousers, shirt and tie and brown leather shoes or boots with a Sam Brown belt and RNAS brass buttons. Rank was still worn on the jacket cuff, but consisted of a cheaper, more durable khaki lace to replace the gold of the standard uniform jacket. In keeping with the influence of the RFC uniform, pilots wore their flying badge over the left breast pocket and above medal ribbons, either in gilt or bronze. Flight commanders' cuff stars were not produced for RNAS khaki uniforms. Khaki cap covers were also acquired to wear over the service dark-blue cap, although some officers had caps made from scratch with fabric-covered peaks.

This uniform was officially sanctioned in November 1916, though this was a mere formality as the practice of wearing khaki on the Western Front was already well established. For RNAS officers serving in the Mediterranean and Africa, tropical dress was essentially identical to the Overseas Service Dress, but could be worn with a white Wolseley helmet or the standard service cap in white or khaki. Once in theatre, many pilots adopted the more practical rig of khaki shorts and shirts with rolled-up sleeves. Pilots serving operationally also wore fibre identity tags, a red disc and a green octagon, both on a length of string around the neck and stamped with the owner's name, service number and religion.

For more formal occasions, the use of Mess Dress for naval officers continued throughout the war. Mess kit comprised of a dark-blue, waist-length, double-breasted jacket with three brass buttons on each side and gold rank lace on the sleeve, worn with the flying badge and stars on the cuff. The jacket was fastened by two brass buttons, secured together with a small link of chain. It became common practice for officers to detach one of these buttons and swap it with an officer in any other service, be it the Army or foreign navies, with whom they may have worked at any point. Miniature medals were worn on the left lapel of the jacket. The jacket was worn over a white shirt with winged collar and gold studs and a black bow tie, together with high-waist trousers and a waistcoat

Five officers in mixed rig aboard the SS *Namur*. The pilot second from the right wears Daily Working Rig with RNAS grey flannel trousers. The officer second from the left wears tropical whites.

tailored in the same colour and material as the jacket; black leather boots completed the uniform.

Specialized flying clothing itself was still very much in its infancy and it was not until the end of the war that purpose-manufactured flying kit was issued to military aviators. By 1916 many aircraft were capable of reaching altitudes above 20,000ft (6,100m), where in winter months temperatures below -40°C were not uncommon. This, in an open-cockpit aircraft and often without the benefits of an aircraft-fitted oxygen-feed system, put considerable physiological pressures on aircrew. Already suffering from the initial effects of hypoxia, flying in these conditions without proper flying clothing would be fatal.

Initially, without the benefit of purpose-designed flying kit, pilots were forced to look elsewhere for equipment and clothing that could easily be used in aviation – motorsports, in particular motorcycling, provided a ready source of leather helmets, gloves and goggles. Manufacturers such as Burberry's, Gieves and Selfridges produced the more desirable 'designer' leather goods, and it was not long until fashion-conscious aviators sought to outdo each other by purchasing the best branded items of flying clothing. The basic essentials were a helmet and goggles, sturdy gauntlets, boots and a flying jacket or coat. During summer and at low altitudes this would suffice, but for braving the extremes of the winter cold, much more protection was required.

The majority of aviators of the era considered goggles rudimentary, but many scout pilots preferred to fly without them, considering anything that could impede vision as an unacceptable detriment. However, aircraft were capable of speeds well in excess of 100mph (161km/h) by the time air-to-air combat began in earnest over the Western Front, and with only a small windscreen fitted to most aircraft and with the added hazards of wind chill lowering the already-cold temperatures, many pilots not only relied on goggles but also brought a spare pair with them into the cockpit. As goggles would quickly become smeared and dirty with oil from the engine, pilots also took to wearing silk scarves so as to have a suitable material for cleaning their goggles readily to hand; the silk scarf became one of the trademark garments of World War I pilots. Goggles designed specifically for military aviation were soon in production, with thicker 'safety' lenses, fur lining and tinted lenses to help spot 'the Hun in the sun'.

SCOUT PILOT, 1917

Dressed for lower-altitude flying in the more forgiving summer months, this pilot wears the minimum clothing necessary in an open-cockpit aircraft over his Daily Working Rig. Being stationed on the Western Front, he wears the single-breasted jacket and trousers of the Officers' Overseas Service Dress. Whilst this part of the uniform was standard by 1917, there was still very little available in terms of issue flying clothing. This pilot wears a privately purchased, lightweight leather coat for warmth in the cockpit. This coat would be of no use in the harsher winter months, and a second, fur-lined garment would be necessary to be worn over many layers of clothing. Also privately purchased are the pilot's helmet, goggles, gloves and boots, all of which are simple adaptations of the protective clothing designed for motorcyclists. Finally, this pilot wears what had already become the signature garment of the pioneer aviator: an oil-stained silk scarf. Whereas silk cravats were favoured in World War II to protect the neck from chafing on a starched collar whilst turning the head to look for enemy aircraft, World War I pilots had more immediate problems. Early aero engines were notoriously dirty, leaving the pilot's goggles streaked with oil and making the silk scarf a necessity rather than a luxury to act as a soft cleaning cloth. The pilot also carries a Webley MkVI service revolver in his boot; whilst of some limited use for self defence if downed behind enemy lines, some pilots considered the primary reason for carrying a pistol was to offer a quick death by shooting oneself in the head if trapped in a burning aircraft at a time when parachutes were prohibited.

Nine naval aircrew officers dressed for winter. Greatcoats and privately purchased flying coats, gloves and scarves are worn over Daily Working Rig.

An RNAS cold-weather flying helmet, 1916. With temperatures at height in an open-cockpit aircraft being well below freezing, functionality had to take priority over fashion.

Helmets were designed not only for protection in the event of impact, but also for extra warmth to help combat the loss of heat from the head. The Roold helmet, which was standard issue for French pilots, was also available commercially and proved popular with RNAS pilots. It consisted of a cloth-covered cork shell with ear flaps. Other manufacturers soon copied the design. More popular with scout pilots was the simple leather motoring-style helmet, which was lighter and did not impede vision. Early in the war pilots would modify this by sewing strips to the side of the helmet to keep goggles in place and prevent them from being blown off by the wind and slipstream in open cockpits, but manufacturers soon implemented this as a standard feature. For cold-weather flying, masks were also available that could button or buckle onto helmets to protect the pilot's face. In the absence of a mask, pilots would

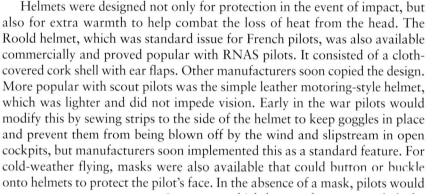

sometimes smear thick layers of grease or whale fat onto their faces to provide a barrier against the vicious effects of wind chill.

Communications in any open-cockpit aircraft proved to be all but impossible as shouting over the combined din of the engine and the howl of the wind was simply inaudible through the thick layers of protection provided by headgear. One device developed by the RFC and soon adopted by the RNAS was the Gosport tube, named after the Hampshire town where the RFC's School of Special Flying was based. The Gosport tube was a simple length of rubber tubing that was connected to the ears of the flying helmet, whilst the other end was connected to the face mask of the aircraft's other crew member. This reliable device was first designed for tuition, so that instructors could shout commands to student pilots. The design was soon incorporated into multi-crew aircraft to allow a pilot and observer to talk to each other, though in training aircraft only the instructor was given the facility to 'transmit' – the student could only 'receive'.

The simplicity of an early war cockpit is evident in this photograph from the pilot's seat of a Blériot Parasol. The only instruments available to pilots were crude speedometers, clocks, balance indicators and engine-oil indicators.

Flying jackets were amongst the first items of official flying clothing, with knee-length, double-breasted leather coats in black chrome-tanned leather being manufactured for the RNAS. These were often worn over issue greatcoats and several layers of thick clothing and underwear, with pilots donning their flying clothing at the last possible moment, as sweat would freeze at altitude. The first purpose-built, issue flying suit was not available to the RNAS until March 1918 – the Sidcot suit. This consisted of overalls of a thin Burberry material lined with fur and silk.

Also available were electrically heated suits designed for bomber crews, made up of a Burberry waistcoat, gloves and boot soles heated by a wind-driven generator. These proved unpopular as the wiring often cracked and failed, and if the aircraft dived and speed increased, the generators too would speed up, sometimes heating the gloves and boots to the point of burning the wearer.

Specific to the naval aviator, various designs of buoyancy aid were also developed. Kapok-lined jackets were available commercially, or simple flotation waistcoats that could be inflated orally. The final item of safety equipment available to some aviators was the parachute. Early parachutes weighed upward of 15kg and were very cumbersome and almost impossible to fit into the cockpit of smaller aircraft types. Parachutes were available to balloon and airship crews, but throughout the war (even after the invention of the smaller, seat-cushion type parachute) pilots of heavier-than-air aircraft were still denied their use. The official line was: 'Possession of a parachute might impair a pilot's nerve when in difficulties so that he would make improper use of his parachute.' In short, pilots were accused of cowardice and were not given any means

Three RNAS pilots model a selection of high-altitude flying clothing. In sub-zero temperatures, aircrew would often smear whale fat on their faces as a further layer of protection from the cold.

The pilot of a Sopwith Pup hurries to extract himself from his cockpit after a failed approach to HMS *Argus*. The wood-and-canvas aircraft would stay afloat for far longer than the metal aircraft that would soon replace them.

to escape a doomed aircraft. For this reason, many pilots were forced to take into the aircraft the only alternative – a revolver – so as to grant themselves a quick death rather than burning alive in a wooden aircraft coated in flammable dope and paint and housing large quantities of fuel, oil and ammunition.

AIRCRAFT OF THE FLEET

The RNAS operated a myriad of aircraft in many different roles throughout World War I. Detailed below is a small selection of some of the more famous or remarkable aircraft to serve during the period.

Avro 504

Serving the RNAS, RFC and RAF as a basic trainer from 1914 until the late 1920s, the Avro 504 was perhaps the most iconic and successful trainer of the pioneering age of aviation. Powered by either an 80bhp Gnome or Le Rhone engine, the 504 was capable of only 82mph (132km/h) at sea level, but possessed stable and forgiving handling characteristics, which made it ideal as both a pilot trainer and a steady platform for delivering ordnance. It is in this latter role that the Avro 504 is often overlooked, but first rose to fame within the RNAS when three 504s bombed the Zeppelin hangars at Freidrichshafen on 21 November 1914. In March 1915 five Avro 504s of No.1 Naval Squadron bombed the submarine base at Hoboken, destroying two U-boats.

Capable of being fitted with a Lewis gun firing up through the centre section of the upper wing, the RNAS also employed the Avro 504 in the anti-Zeppelin role, although in practice the four 20lb bombs also carried often proved to be more effective than the gun against enemy airships. When kitted out as an interceptor or bomber the 504 was flown as a single-seat aircraft. Although by the end of the war the Avro 504 had been replaced as a bomber and interceptor, it continued to excel as a trainer and was also involved in the first arrested deck-landing trials and early experiments in catapult launching.

An RNAS pilot is pushed out to position for launch in an Avro 504. Like so many two-seaters of the era, the 504 had a sensitive centre of gravity, and so had to be flown from the rear seat when only one pilot was onboard.

BELOW
An Avro 504 overflies a Short Type 184 seaplane. The Type 184 was used extensively throughout the war, and was to the RNAS what the Swordfish would be to the Fleet Air Arm in World War II.

De Havilland 4

The DH4 was one of the most outstanding light bombers of the war, and was used extensively by the RFC across several fronts. Service with the RNAS was a little more limited, being used to equip five squadrons along the Western Front and three units at coastal air stations in the UK. Fitted with a selection of differing power plants rated between 200 and 375bhp, the DH4 possessed a good performance, even with its bomb load of up to 430lbs (195kg), which could also be replaced with depth charges. For air-to-air combat, the DH4 was armed with one or two forward-firing Vickers machine guns, and a flexibly mounted Lewis machine gun in the rear cockpit; both gun types were .303 calibre.

Whilst the DH4 was better known for its success as a bomber, it was also very dangerous to enemy scouts in the right hands. Flight Lieutenant Euan Dickson of No.5 Naval Squadron shot down 14 enemy aircraft whilst piloting a DH4. All of his victories were against single-seat scouts.

The first naval squadrons to receive the DH4 were No.2 Naval Squadron at St Pol in March 1917, and No.5 Naval Squadron at Coudekerque a month later. Home-based DH4s achieved several successes, including the shooting down of Zeppelin L70 and the sinking of submarine UB-12, though both of these feats were achieved after the coastal-based squadrons had been handed over to the newly formed RAF.

Short Type 184

Whilst overshadowed by the more 'glamorous' fighting aircraft used on the Western Front, the Short Type 184 seaplane was undoubtedly one of the most influential maritime aircraft of World War I. The RNAS used over 900 Type 184s, which first entered service in 1915. The aircraft came about as a result of Commodore Sueter calling for a powerful seaplane capable of carrying a torpedo. With the first production models being equipped with a 225bhp engine (increasing to 275bhp by the end of its career) the Type 184 was certainly powerful by contemporary standards. Laden with a two-man crew, a Lewis machine gun and a 14in. torpedo, the Type 184 was capable of a top speed of only 88mph (142km/h).

The Type 184 wasted no time in proving Sueter's theories about the potential of a torpedo-carrying aircraft. The first Type 184s in service with the RNAS were embarked aboard the seaplane carrier HMS *Ben-my-Chree* and served in the Dardanelles campaign from June of 1915. On 12 August Flight Commander Edmonds became the first pilot ever to sink a ship at sea with a torpedo when he attacked a 5,000-ton Turkish merchantman in the Gulf of Xeros. He repeated the success only five days later when he torpedoed and disabled a steamer. The Type 184 served with great success in the Mediterranean theatre, being employed in reconnaissance, gunnery spotting and inland bombing. The Type 184 was also used in home waters for anti-submarine patrols, and was in addition the only aircraft used at the battle of Jutland. By the end of the war there were still some 300 Type 184s in service, and the last squadron to replace the aircraft was 202 Squadron in 1921.

The cockpit of a late-war Short 184 seaplane. By this stage, the cockpit now has an array of flight and engine instruments. The placing of these instruments also has much more consideration; the compass (vital for instrument and night flying) is prominent on the windscreen.

Felixstowe F.2A

With a wingspan of over 95ft (29m) and a length of 46ft (14m), the Felixstowe F.2A was one of the largest aircraft used by the RNAS during the war. Powered by two 345bhp Rolls Royce Eagle VIII engines, the large flying boat was capable of 95mph (153km/h) and a service ceiling of 9,600ft (2,926m). Its four-man crew were armed with up to seven .303 Lewis guns in various positions along the fuselage, and two 230lb bombs on racks below the wings. With an

The Sopwith Type 860 first flew in December 1914, and was one of the RNAS's first torpedo bombers. It was powered by a 225bhp Sunbeam Mohawk engine, which was particularly powerful in relation to contemporary engines.

29

endurance of six hours, extendable to over nine hours with extra petrol cans carried internally, the F.2A was one of the most effective long-range anti-submarine and anti-Zeppelin aircraft used by the Allies. It entered service late in 1917, with 160 orders having been placed by March 1918, although only just over half of these were completed by the time the armistice was signed.

One of the greatest advances for patrol-aircraft crews available in the F.2A was dual controls; this allowed two pilots to share the workload on long patrols. Understandably apprehensive about the thought of ditching far from home, F.2A crews took to painting their aircraft in vivid and striking colours and patterns in order to make them as noticeable as possible to friendly search aircraft in case complications arose.

Sopwith 1½ Strutter

The 1½ Strutter achieved many historic firsts in its career. It was the first British aircraft to enter service with a synchronizer gear, the first effective two-seat fighter, the first aircraft ever used for strategic bombing and the first two-seat aircraft to launch from a British warship. The aircraft's bizarre name derived from the strut arrangement of attaching the upper wings to the fuselage via a short half strut and a longer strut. This nickname was soon adopted officially.

The long-range Felixstowe F.2A patrol flying boat was used extensively in the last year of the war. This huge aircraft was uncannily manoeuvrable, and on 4 June 1918 four of these flying boats, accompanied by a Curtiss H12, engaged 14 enemy seaplanes in a huge maritime dogfight. One British aircraft was forced down in exchange for six enemy kills.

The 1½ Strutter entered service with the RNAS in February 1916, serving across several theatres as an escort fighter, light bomber, anti-submarine aircraft and reconnaissance platform. Equipped with a 110 or 130bhp Clerget rotary engine, the 1½ Strutter was capable of speeds just in excess of 100mph (161km/h) and had an endurance of four and a half hours. As a bomber, the aircraft was refitted as a single-seat aircraft to save weight, and could carry four 65lb bombs, as well as a further 12 bombs internally; two 65lb bombs could be fitted to the two-seat variant. Only about 110 of the 550 aircraft manufactured for the RNAS were built as single-seat bombers. The 1½ Strutter served with 15 countries throughout its operational career, most notably in large numbers with France and the United States. Altogether, nearly 6,000 were built, mainly under licence in France.

Nieuport Scouts

The French company Nieuport produced a range of highly effective single-seat scouts throughout the war, all of a similar design and building on the success of their respective predecessor. The first of these to be used in large numbers was the Nieuport 11, which entered service with the RNAS in early 1916, with No.1 Wing in Belgium and No.2 Wing in the Aegean.

The Nieuport 11 was a small, agile scout with an 80bhp Le Rhone rotary engine and a single Lewis gun fitted to the upper wing. The Nieuport's lower wing had a much shorter chord than the upper, helping to maintain a light, manoeuvrable frame but leaving the weak lower wing prone to bending under stress, or even detaching completely in a steep dive. Nieuport 11s could also be fitted with Le Prieur rockets on the struts, which were used against balloons and Zeppelins.

The Sopwith 1½ Strutter was a good fighting platform, but too stable to make a manoeuvrable dogfighter. Its long range and all-round armament made it a good escort fighter, but it stood little chance against German scouts such as the Albatros by 1917.

In November 1916, the improved Nieuport 17bis entered service. It was slightly larger and more powerful, fitted first with a 110 and then 130bhp Clerget engine, giving a maximum speed of 115mph (185km/h). Compared to its contemporaries, the 17bis was again an excellent scout with enviable manoeuvrability and rate of climb, but still suffered from the same structural problem of the weak lower wing. Some 80 were used by the RNAS, often in mixed squadrons alongside Sopwith Pups. The Nieuport line of V-strutted single-seat scouts continued up to the Nieuport 27, which was popular with the RFC; the Nieuport 21 saw limited service with the RNAS, but by the end of 1916 the Sopwith Pup and Triplane proved more popular with naval squadrons.

Sopwith Pup

Originally known as the Sopwith Scout, the Pup was developed in 1915 as a progression from a light aircraft built as the 'Hack' (or personal transport) of Sopwith test pilot Harry Hawker. The small, light Pup was an extremely agile aircraft in possession of pleasing flying characteristics, capable of a maximum speed of some 105mph (169km/h). This was quite an achievement considering its Le Rhone engine supplied only 80bhp. One notable weakness of the Pup was its solitary .303 Vickers machine gun; several German fighters equipping front-line squadrons at the same time were already equipped with two machine guns.

Flight Sub-Lieutenant W. K. F. G. Warneford, related to R. A. J. Warneford, VC, poses by a Nieuport Scout, wearing Overseas Service Dress. He survived the war with the Air Force Cross, transferring over to the RAF before being tragically killed when HM Airship NS11 was lost off Sheringham on 14 July 1919.

A Nieuport 12 of No.1 Wing RNAS at Dunkirk. In the absence of the dual-control system fitted to two-seat trainers, the rear cockpit had to be loaded with counter-balance weights to allow the aircraft to fly with only a single pilot.

A Nieuport 24 Scout of 6 Naval Squadron, attached to the RFC. Some Nieuport 24s were built under licence in England specifically for the RNAS, but by the time they were in squadron service the much more capable Sopwith Camel was also in production.

The Pup first saw trials with Naval 'A' Squadron at Furnes in May 1916, and went on to serve with distinction over the Western Front in providing merchant-shipping protection and in the anti-airship role. It achieved notable world firsts by taking off from a 20ft (6.1m) platform attached to HMS *Yarmouth* in June 1917, and then as the first aircraft ever to land on an aircraft carrier aboard HMS *Furious* in August of the same year. Pups were also the first wheel-equipped aircraft to be operated from seaplane carriers, being fitted with flotation bags to the lower wing for alighting alongside the carrier. Sopwith Pups enjoyed a successful career during World War I, and, although they were outclassed by the more modern German fighters by late 1917, they served with the RNAS until its dissolution.

A Sopwith Pup armed with Le Prieur rockets. The rockets were fired electrically by a switch in the cockpit, and were designed to be used against balloons and airships. Whilst moderately successful against balloons, the adoption of tracer and incendiary rounds by the end of the war made these inaccurate rockets obsolete.

A Sopwith Pup is hoisted aboard HMS *Furious* in 1917. The aircraft's forgiving handling characteristics made it ideal for early deck-landing trials.

Sopwith Triplane

Although not adopted by the RFC, the Sopwith Triplane achieved great successes in its brief career with the RNAS. The extra lift generated by a third wing gave the 'Tripehound' an enviable rate of climb (it took only 22 minutes to reach 16,000ft, or 4,877m) and its relatively short wings also conferred a good roll rate – an invaluable quality for the dogfights of pioneering aerial combat. The wing configuration also gave a great field of view from the cockpit. The Triplane did, however, suffer from the same modest armament as the Pup with its single Vickers machine gun. Equipped with a 130bhp Clerget engine, it was nearly 10mph (16km/h) faster than its smaller stablemate.

Erbeuteter Englischer-Sopwith-Dreidecker

A German propaganda photo of a captured Sopwith Triplane. The introduction of this model impressed German aircraft manufacturers so much that 34 prototype triplanes were produced in Germany. This aircraft has had its roundels and registration number cut away as souvenirs, possibly by the pilot who shot it down.

The Triplane followed the Pup to Furnes for trials with Naval 'A' Squadron in June 1916 before then going on to enter service in February 1917. It served with the RNAS for only seven months before being replaced by the Camel, but built up an envious combat record during this short period. The Triplane served as a seat for 60-kill ace Raymond Collishaw, who scored 34 of his victories whilst flying this type. His 'Black Flight' of 10 Naval Squadron became the scourge of the Western Front at a time when German pilots had up until that point achieved air supremacy in many areas; the black-cowled Triplanes scored 87 confirmed kills between May and July 1917, with Collishaw accounting for 16 kills in just 27 days.

Despite proving popular with pilots, the Sopwith Triplane was notoriously difficult to maintain, often requiring disassembly of the wings or fuselage for relatively minor maintenance. The 'Tripehound', as it was nicknamed, was replaced by the Camel.

Sopwith Camel

Although its combat career was only a little over a year long, the Sopwith Camel was credited with destroying 1,294 enemy aircraft, more than any other Allied fighter of the war. Its extreme agility was in part due to its engine, pilot, fuel tank and guns all being squeezed in to the front of the aircraft; this was, however, a double-edged sword. Whilst the Camel possessed an enviable reputation in combat, it was also known for its difficult handling characteristics and a particularly vicious spin, both of which were responsible for the deaths of an inordinate number of student pilots. Due to the powerful torque reaction of the Camel's rotary engine, it turned sluggishly to the left but quicker than any contemporary aircraft to the right, and its heavy tail also produced a fast loop.

By summer 1917, it was Britain's turn to produce aircraft that would be the scourge of the Western Front. The deadly Sopwith Camel was universally feared by its enemies, shooting down more aircraft than any other Allied type. Royal Navy pilots alone accounted for 386 confirmed kills whilst flying Camels.

Equipped with either a 130bhp Clerget or 150bhp Bentley engine, the Camel's top speed was a mere 115mph (185km/h) or 118mph (190km/h) respectively. Its rate of climb was less than the Sopwith Triplane and its handling characteristics were certainly less pleasant and forgiving than its two predecessors. It was, however, far more manoeuvrable and had twice the punch with two Vickers .303 machine guns, or one Vickers and one Lewis gun on the 2F.1 naval variant. It first entered service in June 1917 with No.4 Squadron of the RNAS, near Dunkirk. This was also the first Camel squadron to see action and claim kills, early the next month.

The 2F.1 variant of the Camel onboard HMS *Furious* in 1918. The temperamental Camel was a more difficult aircraft to handle at sea than the Pup it replaced.

The aforementioned 2F.1 variant of the Camel was designed from the outset as a shipborne fighter, with its fuselage being constructed in two sections so that it could be disconnected as a space-saving measure at sea. Maritime Camels were used primarily as Zeppelin interceptors, being flown off platforms attached to the gun turrets of large warships, from the decks of carriers or from small lighters towed behind destroyers. After the war, Camels took part in early arrested deck-landing trials onboard HMS *Argus*.

ON CAMPAIGN: CONDITIONS IN THEATRE

Although RNAS pilots served in most theatres of World War I, in varying living conditions, there can be no doubt that the day-to-day living arrangements provided for an RNAS officer were more comfortable than those experienced by their brethren in the front-line branches of the Army. Perhaps the most fortunate in this respect were those who were stationed on the home front; for them, their 'theatre' was the UK itself. Upon completion of training, T. D. Hallam was sent to Felixstowe Air Station in March 1917 – the station was, as with all Royal Navy shore establishments, run as much as possible in the same way as a warship. Duty personnel were split into watches,

An aerial photograph of RNAS Cranwell in March 1918. It had been opened the previous year as a training establishment for the RNAS, but with the formation of the RAF in April 1918 it was converted into the training base for RAF officers.

timings were run off a ship's bell and leaving the station was referred to as 'going ashore'. The 'quarterdeck' was a large, flat area of tarmac dominated by a tall ship's mast which flew the Royal Navy ensign. In the morning and at noon divisions were piped, and all available 'Ship's Company' would muster on the quarterdeck in smart rig, marching to the tune of a pipe band, if the occasion demanded.

Pilots were accommodated with other officers in the station wardroom. Wardrooms on the home front, especially in the older naval establishments, were typically grandiose affairs, with officers accommodated in single-man 'cabins', silver service meals in formal rig being provided every night and public rooms such as reading rooms, games rooms and the bar often decorated with grand paintings of past naval actions. The daily working routine for flying-boat pilots at Felixstowe was fairly slow in comparison to other theatres; weather and aircraft serviceability often prevented anti-U-boat patrols from becoming a daily occurrence, leaving pilots with a lot of time on their hands. Much of this time was taken up in test flying newly manufactured flying boats. The patrols themselves were also fairly slow paced, with only two U-boats being sighted by aircraft based from Felixstowe in the first two years of the war. By 1917 this pace had picked up considerably, and the work carried out by the flying-boat crews of Felixstowe became invaluable to the safety of merchant shipping bringing vital supplies into Britain.

Conditions on the Western Front were far from the comforts experienced by the seaplane pilots based in England, but still much better than life in the trenches. Naval tradition and terminology was still strongly encouraged by most commanding officers, with anything outside of the aerodrome boundary being referred to as 'ashore' and ceremonial divisions still being carried out as best as possible on Sundays. Depending on where a squadron was based and for how long, pilots would be accommodated at their airfield in either tents or wooden huts, or would be billeted to local houses with any family willing to put them up. Again, most pilots could expect single accommodation

Accommodation of a probationary flight sub-lieutenant in Eastbourne, January 1918. The airfield at RNAS Eastbourne was used for initial pilot training throughout the war.

afforded to them due to their status as officers, although sharing a tent or hut with another pilot was not unheard of. Charles Bartlett shared his cabin in Flanders in September 1916 with another squadron officer; he recalled the atmosphere and camaraderie very favourably, and recorded in his diary details of how the two put in much effort to transform their bland cabin into something more homely, with new wallpaper, curtains, furniture, a rug and photographs from home.

Flight Lieutenant Harold Rosher of No.1 Naval Aeroplane Squadron was attached to the BEF in March 1915. He was stationed in a large house with seven others from his squadron, five minutes from a public bath and in conditions that he described in his letters home as being very comfortable. His letters home did, however, often request amenities such as literature or tobacco, which was hard to come by so close to the front line. Also sent from home were more essential items such as new uniforms and flying clothing. Letters to and from home formed a huge part of the lives of servicemen of all branches and trades in every theatre of the war, and every effort was

A pilot poses in front of his Sopwith Pup. During warmer summer months pilots could wear a leather coat, boots, helmet and gloves over the top of their Daily Working Rig, without the need for the several layers of fur necessary during winter.

taken to deliver these letters quickly and safely, as they had such a huge effect on morale. Whilst families in Belgium and France were most hospitable to the British pilots and their ground crews, the transient nature of air warfare meant that squadrons would often pack up and move at very short notice, often to the next in a series of makeshift aerodromes cobbled together out of the largest and flattest field that could be acquired. Whilst Rosher never complained of the hospitality of the local families, he described one aerodrome as 'beastly' and an accident waiting to happen. Because of the short range of aircraft of the period, aerodromes were situated very close to the front lines, often close enough for the artillery of both sides to be audible if the wind was in the right direction.

For entertainment, pilots would often travel as a squadron to their local town in search of the traditional attractions to young men on foreign soil in military service – women and alcohol. Short periods of leave could be spent in Paris if not enough time was allocated to travel to the UK and back, giving some pilots a break from front-line service in the bright lights of a big city, relatively safe and far away from enemy guns. Leave was, unfortunately, a rare commodity as pilots were in demand throughout the course of the war.

The conditions endured by pilots on the Western Front were not unique to the RNAS; the RFC (and for that matter pilots of the German Flying Corps) shared these living conditions, a fact which allowed a fraternity of aviators to emerge which sometimes blurred the rules of fraternization. Much legend and myth has emerged with regards to the chivalry displayed by pilots of both sides during World War I, although there is certainly enough evidence to prove that a bond of sorts did exist between pilots on both sides of the lines. Squadron Commander Chris Draper of the notorious 'Naval 8' scout squadron recorded a curious incident in September 1917, when a German aircraft dropped a message on his aerodrome at St Eloi, giving details of British pilots recently killed or captured, and politely requesting the favour to be reciprocated. Whilst no quarter was shown in the air, it was considered good form on both sides to throw a party for any enemy airman safely downed on the wrong side of the lines, to give them a final send off before being sent to a prisoner-of-war camp.

Whilst the air war on the Western Front captured much of the public's attention, the RNAS was also heavily involved in the fighting against Turkey during the Dardanelles campaign. Eugene Gerrard, one of the original four navy fliers in 1911, took his scout squadron to the theatre:

> Although the campaign was a failure, it was extremely interesting from our point of view... We could see the whole War in five minutes and we dabbled in everything: Bombing, Reconnaissance, Photography, Fighting, and anti-submarine work. The latter was rather disappointing; I hoped to be able to see a submerged submarine, in the relative clear of the Mediterranean Sea, but it became invisible a few feet down... There was not much in the way of fighting till a section of Richthoven's [sic] Circus arrived.

Without the same opportunities for entertainment in local towns and cities that pilots on the Western Front could enjoy, the RNAS pilots on the Dardanelles campaign had to create their own excitement. Gerrard wrote: 'The Turkish anti-aircraft fire was very poor. Young Munday, who was a camera fiend, often had to turn towards the shell bursts to get a good photograph!'

Away from their primary duties of flying, pilots of the RNAS were, like any other naval officers, expected to carry out a number of secondary duties. Most important of these was the duty of divisional officer. The squadron's ratings were split into groups, or divisions, each placed under the charge of one officer. Within these divisions, this officer was responsible for the administration and well-being of the ratings placed in his charge. Pilots would be expected to have a large input into the career progression and promotion recommendations of junior and senior ratings in their division, and if any of their ratings were 'trooped' for disciplinary offences, the divisional officer would act as the 'accused's friend' at any subsequent hearing. Other secondary duties would be handed out to individuals by the more senior members of the squadron; these duties included jobs such as mess wine accounts officer, maps and charts officer or squadron socials officer; the list of secondary duties would vary from squadron to squadron at the behest of the commanding officer.

Even though a great number of RNAS pilots were 'hostilities only' officers who joined the Royal Navy because it was wartime, there were still a great many career-minded individuals who saw the RNAS as their vocation, not just their way of doing their part for the war effort. Advancement followed a very strict set of guidelines, with officers being reported on by their immediate superiors with regards not only to their performance in the air and in action

The Sopwith Tabloid – winner of the Monaco Schnieder Trophy in 1914. In October 1914 the RNAS used two of its three Tabloids to attack the Zeppelin sheds at Cologne and Dusseldorf. Flight Lieutenant Matrix successfully found his target, destroying the new Zeppelin ZIX in its shed.

with the enemy, but also in the course of carrying out their ground-based duties, and, very importantly, their responsibilities as a divisional officer. Commanding officers would send their list of promotion recommendations to the promotions board at the Admiralty, where those selected would be duly informed via a routine signal promulgated amongst the squadrons. Charles Bartlett's diary entry for 1 July 1917 makes very obvious references to his anger at not being selected for promotion to flight lieutenant, with more junior officers, whom he described as 'slackers' with 'cushy safe jobs' on the home front, being promoted ahead of him. Whilst it would be completely unfair to speculate whether these men on the home front were any less deserving of promotion, it was often the case that reports or promotion recommendations were delayed or lost entirely in the long administration chain leading from the front line to the Admiralty.

Whilst conditions on the front line would never be comfortable for any combatant of any service during World War I, it was whilst actually airborne that RNAS pilots could potentially encounter the worst conditions. Those perhaps subject to the most variable conditions whilst aloft were the crews of the RNAS's balloons and airships. In the cars suspended beneath the airships pilots were completely open to the elements. Thomas Williams recalled the elation of 'stunting' a Submarine Scout Zero airship at low level along the Thames, jumping bridges in the manner of a racehorse to show off to a passenger. Frederick Verry, another RNAS airship man, remembered flying his airship back home 'like a motor boat' on fine-weather days, just allowing the car to touch the surface of the water when returning from anti-submarine patrols.

The odd occasion to enjoy the job did little to make up for the poor working conditions endured by RNAS airship pilots and their crews. In the harsh winter months, patrols of many hours were commonplace, in freezing skies, wind, rain and ice. If the temperature and exposure were not enough to endure, even normally simple tasks such as using the toilet were a job in themselves, with the only toilet facilities on the long-endurance airships being a length of rubber hose attached to a hole in the bottom of the car. The airship pilot's war was a long, cold, thankless and often boring one.

A view rearwards of the control car of HM Airship *C2*. The airship was based at RNAS Howden near York, which opened in June 1916 to provide anti-submarine patrols around the ports of the East Coast.

BELIEF AND BELONGING

The motivation that spurred an individual to volunteer for a career in military aviation varied from person to person, but there are certainly trends that emerge from firsthand accounts of the period. During World War I an overriding patriotism pushed many men to volunteer for military service, often before it became compulsory, but it took a certain type of character to then consider a career as an aviator.

Aviation appealed to those drawn from civilian life and those already in the service alike; by the outbreak of war, powered heavier-than-air aviation had existed for only 11 years, and the great pre-war pioneers of aviation were treated as international heroes and celebrities, lending a rich glamour to flying. For many of those already in the Royal Navy, this seemed like a perfect way to break away from some of the more monotonous or tedious daily working routines associated with the surface fleet.

Air days and air shows up and down the country also acted as a great attraction for potential aviators; Harold Rosher had been bitten by the flying bug early in 1914 when he had flown as a passenger at Brooklands airfield. On the day war was declared, Rosher applied for a commission in the RNAS and then began to pay for his own flying training at Brooklands before the War Office commandeered the aerodrome and gave him a commission as a probationary flight sub-lieutenant. Rosher was tragically killed in 1916, at the

Squadron Commander E. H. Dunning is congratulated moments after the first ever deck landing on a ship underway. He landed a Sopwith Pup on HMS *Furious* on 2 August 1917.

age of 22, flying what is known in modern terms as a 'check test flight' – flying an aircraft immediately after a significant repair or period of maintenance. His motivation and loyalty to his squadron and the service right to the very end are evident in the letters he regularly wrote to his family, now publically available.

Also impressed by these early shows of airmanship was Richard Bell-Davies, the only RNAS Victoria Cross recipient to survive the war. Before the outbreak of war, as a watch keeper aboard the battleship HMS *Dominion*, Bell-Davies recalled his emotions at seeing an early flying display when at anchor in Mount's Bay: 'The cheering was spreading from ship to ship... I saw two little lines in the sky low down over the shore. It was Claude Grahame-White in a Farman biplane, heading seawards over the fleet. By that time the whole fleet was yelling... The enthusiasm was tremendous.' So inspired by the display was Bell-Davies that when Frank McLean advertised his two aeroplanes as being available for the tuition of naval officers who wished to learn to fly, Bell-Davies was one of the first to put his name forward.

Charles Bartlett was similarly inspired by witnessing at first hand the French pioneer Blériot land near Margate in 1912. Despite being rejected medically by the RNAS, as described earlier, Bartlett applied for the RFC but again without success. After overhearing some derogatory remarks at his lack of uniform during a garden party, Bartlett was motivated to apply again, fortunately with success.

Reginald Warneford, another RNAS Victoria Cross recipient, was inspired more by patriotism and a sense of duty rather than the glamour of flying. In January 1915, at the age of 23, Warneford took his place in the queue at one of hundreds of army recruitment centres across the country. When the recruiting sergeant demanded the reasoning behind his motivation for

Tragically, Dunning was killed five days after the first ever deck landing, his aircraft stalling as he attempted to go around from a missed approach. He was knocked unconscious as his Pup hit the water, and drowned before help could arrive.

volunteering for military service, Warneford glanced across to a poster behind the sergeant, depicting a girl handing a white feather to a young man in civilian clothing, adorned with the caption: 'Are you doing your bit?' Warneford replied simply: 'To do my bit.' Quickly becoming disillusioned with army life, undergone in a succession of training establishments in Britain, Warneford applied for a commission in the RNAS, where he hoped to find more excitement and be reacquainted with life at sea after earlier experience on ocean liners.

Once trained and on the operational strength of a front-line RNAS squadron, pilots would invariably find that the war was not in the least bit as glamorous as the exploits of the pre-war pioneers would have led them to believe. The maintenance of motivation and morale became a real struggle for aviators caught up in the vicious and bloody air war that raged across several theatres. Whereas the horrors of trench warfare were, to some small extent, acknowledged by the British Army, no provisions were made for aviators to rest and recuperate after fatigue on the front line. Soldiers were rotated through front-line duties in the trenches in an attempt to provide some rest, but for pilots of the RNAS, like their RFC brethren, patrols and raids were flown day after day with no periods of rest allocated other than their standard leave entitlement, which was often revoked.

The camaraderie that developed at squadron level was often all that existed to maintain morale. Experienced squadron commanders were wary of exhaustion and stress in their longer-serving pilots; the fatigue of long flights in gruelling conditions with no periods of rest, the depression resulting from losing friends regularly and the constant fear of death would have a profound effect on every pilot, no matter how stalwart. In a period where combat fatigue was completely unacknowledged as a serious mental-health issue, squadron commanders could only recommend that their battle-weary pilots be sent home for a period of relative rest as an instructor, away from the front line. Even so, pilots were just as susceptible as their better-documented brethren in the infantry to developing long term mental illnesses from their experiences on the front line. In the end, belief in their cause could not be sustained by the myth of the glory of air combat, or by the fear of receiving white feathers from callous women; individual pilots, like members of every branch of the armed forces, had to believe that they were doing 'their bit'.

D   **AFTER THE BATTLE**

Much has been made of the 'chivalry' afforded between 'knights of the air' of the opposing sides of World War I, in a large part due to popular fiction written after the war. Whereas the majority of primary source material indicates that the war in the air was nothing short of a bloody, deadly and terrifying affair there is still some evidence that a bond of sorts existed between aviators on both sides of the lines. Whilst certainly not an official regulation, it was customary wherever possible to 'dine out' a surviving enemy pilot before he was sent off to a prisoner-of-war camp. This would often involve a simple dinner with the downed pilot as guest of honour, followed by drinks in the mess.

This custom was by no means universal, and would often be at the discretion of the commanding officer of the victorious squadron. There were many pilots who viewed war as just that, and had no desire to fraternize with their enemy. Others, such as Manfred von Richthofen, would happily be photographed alongside their surviving victims. The German word for fighter pilot, *Jägdflieger*, is derived from the word *Jäger* or 'hunter', and that mentality was rife amongst the German scout-pilot fraternity. Roundels, guns, registration numbers and other trophies taken from downed RNAS and RFC aircraft would decorate the officers' mess and quarters of German scout squadrons in the same way hunters boasted of their kills. Manfred von Richthofen even had a dedicated trophy room.

EXPERIENCE OF BATTLE

Whilst it had been a tremendous job in the pre-war Royal Navy to argue the necessity for owning and operating aircraft, it was with the outbreak of hostilities that the RNAS now had to actually prove its usefulness. In 1914, whilst aircraft possessed acceptable performance in terms of range and height, aviators were still hampered by other issues. In the ground-attack role, aircraft were so light and underpowered that bomb loads were minimal at best, and carried inside the cockpit of aircraft to be dropped over the side onto targets. For reconnaissance, the only cameras that had sufficient resolution to be of any use were large, cumbersome glass-plate cameras. Also, for naval gunnery spotting and artillery spotting along the Western Front, radio-telephony had not yet been invented and the only way of communicating with a ship or gun battery was via a heavy Morse-code transmitter; so heavy in fact that early reconnaissance aircraft did not have the power to also carry a receiver, and so communications were only in one direction. At the beginning of the war, the idea of designing an aircraft purely to shoot down enemy aircraft had not yet been thought of, and in the opening weeks of the war aircraft on both sides flew with no defensive armament whatsoever.

The RNAS's first action of the war to attract worldwide attention was the attack on the Cuxhaven Zeppelin sheds on Christmas Day, 1914. The raid achieved almost nothing of military value but many lessons were identified for future operations. The force employed used no real tactics at all – it was literally a case of launching all aircraft and each crew then operating individually in the same target area. There were two large problems with addressing this issue. Firstly, it took a good deal of time to launch a seaplane, and early maritime aircraft did not have the endurance to circle overhead a seaplane carrier whilst waiting for the other aircraft of a strike force to launch. Secondly, communicating between aircraft was very difficult. In the days before radio-telephony from aircraft to aircraft was possible, the only other practical means of communicating was hand signals between crews from their open cockpits. During the Cuxhaven Raid, this too would have been nearly impossible in the thick fog that prevailed, but even in good conditions it would be necessary for aircraft to fly in very tight formations so that there could be no ambiguity in hand signals from other aircraft. It was this requirement to fly and fight as a team that prompted the birth of formation flying.

Formation flying as a discipline was vital for both bomber and scout pilots, as both needed to be able to fight as a unit, rather than individually. The main problem faced by a pilot during formation flying is the correct visual judgement of distance from another aircraft – too far away and hand signals will not be recognized, too close and any aircraft in the formation who manoeuvres suddenly runs the risk of colliding with his wingmen. Early experiments in formation flying developed the same techniques that are used today, including the use of visual reference points on another aircraft. Depending on the pilot's position in a formation and the type of aircraft he is in formation with, this might involve tucking into echelon port (to the left and slightly behind the leader) and then lining up a wing strut with the engine cowling as a forward visual reference, and then similarly lining up the tail skid with a prominent point on the rudder or elevator as an aft point. In theory, if all aircraft in the formation use exactly the same visual reference points, the formation will have even spacing. The problem with this technique in wartime flying is that the pilot cannot allow himself to become fixated on his visual reference points; he

This pilot has added a second Lewis gun to his Nieuport 10 of No.1 Wing, positioned to fire down and to the right of the propeller disc.

needs to be regularly checking his leader for hand signals and, even more importantly, craning his neck and checking all around him for any enemy aircraft. The problems and hazards inherent in formation flying only multiplied as formations grew larger, with more aircraft to add to the potential mayhem and confusion. Without radio telephony this technique was, unfortunately, essential and it would take the hard lessons learned in the early stages of the Battle of Britain in 1940 for the RAF to realize that loose formations were far more practical and flexible, just so long as pilots could still communicate with each other.

A Short Folder type seaplane from HMS *Engadine* in 1917. Three Short Folders were involved in the Cuxhaven Raid. The Short brothers patented the design that allowed aircraft wings to be folded back alongside the fuselage for ease of storage.

Pilots of the RNAS were involved in many notable actions of the war. On 19 November 1915, whilst leading No.3 Squadron, Richard Bell-Davies won the RNAS's second Victoria Cross for his actions near Ferrijik Junction in Bulgaria. Under the direction of C. R. Samson, Bell-Davies led his squadron to carry out long-range bombing raids on the railway junctions at Ferrijik and Burgess Bridge in an attempt to hamper the supply routes from Germany to Turkish forces. During the attack, the Henri Farman piloted by Flight Sub-Lieutenant Gilbert Smylie was hit in the engine and forced down into marshland near the Maritza River. Having already set fire to his machine and seeing that Bell-Davies was in a descent to extract him, Smylie used his pistol to shoot his one remaining bomb in order to destroy it before the flames might detonate it near his squadron commander. With enemy soldiers rapidly approaching,

E   **THE CUXHAVEN RAID**

Determined to take action against the growing threat of German airships, the Admiralty ordered the execution of 'Plan Y' – the attack on the German airship base near Cuxhaven. The plan called for three seaplane carriers, HMS *Engadine*, HMS *Riviera* and HMS *Empress*, escorted by HMS *Arethusa* and HMS *Undaunted* supported by a force of eight destroyers, to sail on 24 December 1914 to launch their aircraft the next morning. Four Short 74s, three Short Folders and two of the new Short 135s, each armed with three 20lb bombs, were lowered into the calm waters; unfortunately, owing to the light winds and bitter chill, only seven aircraft were able to get airborne. Due to the different launch times and aircraft performances, all seven aircraft soon became separated, coasting in across the German shore only to encounter thick banks of fog. Hampered by terrible weather and poor intelligence with regards to their target, not one pilot succeeded in finding the Nordholz airship base. The only deliberate attack made against a confirmed enemy unit was by Flt. Lt. Edmonds, piloting one of the Type 74s. Edmonds, flying at 250ft (76m) to remain screened by the ground, followed the Bremerhaven–Cuxhaven railway before becoming lost and forced to abandon his search for the target. Edmonds emerged in clear skies over the coast near the Weser, where he was fired upon by the cruisers *Stralsund* and *Graudenz*. Edmonds' aircraft was hit six times, but still he pressed on his attack, unfortunately only managing a near miss with one bomb before turning back towards his carrier.

Wreckage of a Sopwith Camel on the Western Front in 1917. A worryingly large proportion of pilots who were killed flying Camels met their deaths in flying accidents long before meeting the enemy, so harsh were Its handling characteristics.

Bell-Davies skilfully piloted his own aircraft down and landed amidst the marshes, keeping clear of the flames and debris from Smylie's Henri Farman. In a bold move, which had never before been attempted, Bell-Davies rescued Smylie by squeezing him in between the rudder bars and engine oil tank before taking to the skies again, moments ahead of the rapidly approaching enemy soldiers. Bell-Davies later described the action modestly: 'It never occurred to me that we were likely to be interfered with by enemy troops... I later learned that Smylie had seen a party of Bulgarian troops approaching... It was no easy matter to accommodate him in my plane as there was no passenger seat... Enemy troops were coming close so I lost no time in taking off... The flight back to base took three-quarters of an hour and I felt sorry for poor Smylie...'

He received the Victoria Cross on 1 January 1916. The citation surmised: 'Squadron Commander Davies descended at a safe distance from the burning machine, took up Sub-Lieutenant Smylie, in spite of the near approach of a party of the enemy, and returned to the aerodrome, a feat of airmanship that can seldom have been equalled for skill and gallantry.' Smylie was awarded the Distinguished Service Order for his own part in the action, having flown his wounded bomber over the target to drop his bombs even after his engine had been hit and disabled.

The RNAS had from its very inception been created as a maritime weapon and so was heavily involved in the pioneering tactics developed in the field of maritime operations. Be it through attacking with mines, bombs or torpedoes, aviators at the beginning of the war were all faced with the same common problem: weight. The 21in. torpedo commonly used by destroyers of the Royal Navy was too heavy for any contemporary aircraft; the lighter 18in. torpedo popular within the submarine service was therefore selected. The next problem encountered was in developing a method of delivery; wings were too fragile to carry ordnance of this size, so torpedo brackets were fitted beneath the belly of a Short Seaplane in 1914 to carry out launching trials. The system adopted was the same that would be used with great success in both world wars – the pilot would fly low over the water, arming and launching the torpedo from levers within the cockpit. The height and speed of the aircraft during launch needed to be within certain windows to ensure the torpedo entered the water at the correct angle, or it could bounce, dive too steeply or somersault. On 28 July 1914, Lieutenant A. M. Longmore successfully launched the first torpedo from an airborne platform. The ideas behind launching torpedoes from aircraft were easily translated to bombs and mines, and effective racks for the latter two types of armament were developed during the early stages of World War I to replace the less effective method of manually dropping bombs out of the cockpit of a bomber.

Whilst not as glamorous to the public as some of the more directly combative roles, maritime reconnaissance was an important task carried out by the RNAS. The ability to see a good 100 miles (161km) over the horizon by launching an organic air asset, which could then communicate via wireless without having to take the time to recover to the deck, was something that many of the 'big gun mentality' warship commanders took time to appreciate. Seaplanes could be carried by seaplane tenders attached to the fleet, which were always present and on hand at short notice to provide this extra capability.

Providence selected a particularly crucial day for this to first be proven: the battle of Jutland, the largest naval battle of the entire war. The Imperial German Navy's High Seas Fleet (Hochseeflotte) clashed with the Grand Fleet of the Royal Navy off the mainland of Denmark from 31 May to 1 June 1916.

Two naval officers stand by a Morane Saulnier monoplane. This aircraft wears the early war markings of a red-and-white roundel alongside a Union Flag. Morane Saulnier Types G and H enjoyed great success before the war as sports aircraft.

Flight Lieutenant F. J. Rutland piloted a Short Type 184 with Assistant Paymaster Trewin as his wireless operator, the only aircraft to be used at Jutland, from the seaplane tender *Engadine*, a veteran of the Cuxhaven Raid. Rutland wrote of his experience after the war:

> I got away in a Short, No.8359... We got off in undisturbed water, sighted the enemy and sent in our reports. They put in some extremely accurate Anti-Aircraft fire, but we took little notice of this. We got our report to Engadine, and although it was arranged they should then be passed by signal to the Lion, the Battle cruiser communications were so badly organised that she would not answer our call, but the signals were picked up by a light Cruiser and passed on.

Clearly passionate about proving the capabilities of the RNAS, Rutland continues: 'Here was perhaps the turning point in the Navy's appreciation of the use to which Aircraft could be used in conjunction with warships... We had established inter-communication between plane and ship, in action, for the first time in history. It was the fault of the Navy entirely that we were not used to better effect.'

Rutland goes on to further criticize command at Jutland. Due to further communications problems, the seaplane carrier HMS *Campania* joined the fleet late, and with a top speed of only 14 knots (26km/h) was unable catch up. As a result, she was ordered to return to port. 'It seems to have escaped the Commander in Chief,' Rutland surmised, 'that even if she were 100 miles [161km] astern, her planes could still operate with the fleet. She had one great advantage, seaplanes could be flown from her decks, she carried fourteen, all equipped with wireless and with thoroughly trained wireless operators.

ZEPPELIN ATTACK

Flight Sub-Lieutenant R. A. J. Warneford attacks Zeppelin LZ37 near Ghent on the night of 7 June 1915. Warneford had launched from Furnes aerodrome at 0100hrs, climbing through the night mist to search for two Zeppelins whose radio transmissions had been intercepted. He found one of the Zeppelins, LZ37, north of Ostend and heading south-east. After pursuing through the mist for some 45 minutes Warneford started a climb to position himself for a bomb attack, but was sighted and fired upon by a gunner aboard the Zeppelin. The airship initiated an ascent in order to deny Warneford's Morane Saulnier Type L the chance to climb above it, and after failing to outclimb the airship as he evaded its gunners Warneford broke off his attack in an attempt to convince the crew of the LZ37 that he had given up.

By 0215hrs the LZ37 was north of Ghent at some 10,000ft (3,048m) and now began to descend for its home aerodrome at Gontronde. Warneford climbed to 11,000ft (3,353m) and manoeuvred directly above the airship before switching his engine off to keep his approach as silent as possible. Warneford dived down onto the airship, releasing his bombs a mere 150ft (46m) above it. The resulting explosion nearly tore the LZ37 in two, sending it falling to the ground in flames. The airship fell onto the St Elisabeth Convent in Ghent, killing two nuns, a child and one man who died attempting to rescue survivors in the burning building. Only one of the 28 crew aboard the LZ37 survived.

The explosion flipped Warneford's Morane Saulnier over onto its back and sent it somersaulting towards the ground, its engine unable to restart. Warneford glided down to land behind enemy lines where he was able to carry out repairs on his machine, reattaching the fuel lines before taking off to fly for home. He was awarded the Victoria Cross and the French equivalent, the Légion d'honneur. He became something of a celebrity from his exploits, but was killed only ten days later when his Farman F27 suffered structural failure and flipped over. Neither Warneford nor his passenger, an American journalist, were wearing their safety belts, and both were flung out of the aircraft from a height of about 700ft (213m).

The Short Type 184 was the first aircraft to sink an enemy ship with a torpedo. Early torpedo-carrying aircraft were constrained to the lighter 14in. torpedo until heavier, more powerful aircraft were developed.

Many of the mistakes at Jutland would have been averted had she been present.' The disappointment of the *Campania*'s crews aside, the solitary seaplane launched at Jutland proved, under fire, that in the RNAS the Royal Navy had another valuable weapon in its arsenal.

As soon as aviators on both sides began to achieve success in reconnaissance and bombing, the natural progression was for crews to try to devise techniques and tactics to hinder or stop enemy machines from carrying out their duties. There is plenty of anecdotal evidence to support stories of aviators in the opening weeks of the war simply waving at the crews of enemy aircraft in passing, but soon pilots and observers began arming themselves in an attempt to damage or destroy their opposition. This first came in the form or simple projectiles such as darts, grenades, bricks and even lengths of rope to foul an enemy machine's propeller. Soon, this progressed on to crews carrying pistols and rifles to shoot at other machines, but it was only when machine guns came into play that the idea of a fighting aircraft was born.

Ironically, it was forward-thinking minds within the Admiralty that were amongst the first in the world to predict this progression when, in 1912, the Admiralty placed a contract with Vickers to design and build an experimental fighting biplane armed with a machine gun. Vickers were faced with the obvious problem of how to prevent a forward-firing machine gun from shooting off one's own propeller; they overcame this by using a 'pusher' aircraft (one with a propeller fitted behind the pilot, pushing the aircraft instead of pulling it via the now more traditional 'tractor' method of having the propeller at the front of the aircraft) and fitting a machine gun on a flexible mount in a nacelle in front of the engine. Whilst the theory was fine, the Vickers EFB 1 test flew in 1913 where it briefly left the ground and then nosed over and flipped onto its back due to being too nose-heavy with the gun. The idea was sound, however, and both the RNAS and RFC began to receive pusher-type fighting aircraft armed with forward-firing machine guns, such as the Vickers FB5 'Gunbus'. There was one significant disadvantage of the pusher-type configuration – the fuselage was less streamlined and extra struts and wires were necessary to fix the tail in place, causing a good deal of additional drag and in turn reducing speed and performance.

A second method of producing an effective fighting aircraft was the use of the synchronizer gear. This involved fitting a fixed machine gun to a conventional, tractor-type aircraft with the gun fitted in front of the pilot but behind the propeller, usually on top of the engine. The synchronizer gear attached the propeller shaft to the gun's trigger via a cam, thus only allowing the gun to fire when the propeller blades were clear. This idea had been devised, tested and patented before the war, but had not been perfected to anywhere near a safe level. The Frenchman Roland Garros famously took to the skies in April 1915 with an even simpler system: metal plates were fitted to his propeller to deflect bullet strikes. Whilst he did claim a number of downed enemy aircraft, engine problems – possibly from the shock loading of bullets repetitively striking his own propeller – forced him to land behind German lines, and his aircraft was captured before he could destroy it. It was then sent on to Anthony Fokker, a Dutchman who designed aircraft for Germany. Fokker developed the existing idea of the synchronizer gear and fitted it to his own aircraft. Whilst the Fokker 'Eindecker' series of monoplanes were by no means outstanding aircraft, the inclusion of an effective synchronizer gear allowed this machine to dominate the Western Front, and August 1915 saw the opening round of the 'Fokker Scourge', where Germany achieved air superiority over the British and French.

Morane Saulnier Type L No.3253 – the aircraft used by R. A. J. Warneford to win his Victoria Cross. Roland Garros used the same type of aircraft when he fitted deflector plates to his propeller blades to allow for a forward-firing machine gun.

It was not until 1916 that British and French pilots were equipped with aircraft types able to fight back against the 'Fokker Scourge'. The RFC relied on the pusher type, using DH2s and FE2bs. The RNAS, however, ordered the French Nieuport 11, a tractor-engine biplane, which it used to equip No.1 Wing of the RNAS in Belgium and No.2 Wing in the Aegean. Whilst still not fitted with a synchronizer gear, the Nieuport 11 overcame this by fitting a Lewis machine gun on the upper wing, fixed to fire forwards but above and clear of the propeller. The nimble Nieuport 11 was more than a match for the Fokker Eindecker, and RNAS scout pilots now had a machine to reclaim the skies over Belgium and France. The first synchronizer gear fitted to aircraft to see service with the RNAS was the Sopwith 1½ Strutter, a heavier two-seat fighting aircraft that also entered service in early 1916. Germany now began developing the first aircraft designed with the sole purpose of shooting down enemy aircraft. The introduction of the Albatros series of scout aircraft transferred air superiority back to Germany, and this constant shifting of aerial dominance in correlation with who had the most advanced type of scout would continue until the Armistice.

Air-to-air combat had now become a very real part of military aviation. What had just a few months before consisted of opposing machines taking pot shots at each other with pistols and rifles had, by 1917, evolved into entire aircraft designed from the drawing board exclusively as air-to-air fighters. Fast, agile dogfighters with two machine guns were now ruling the skies over the Western Front, and with this evolution in machinery came huge leaps in the tactics employed to maximize their effectiveness.

The first step in establishing tactics was teamwork; the early-war aces such as Max Immelmann and Oswald Boelcke had scored their first kills whilst flying alone, but it was Boelcke, the 'Father of Air-Fighting Tactics', who realized that air combat pilots needed guidance and rules. His *Dicta Boelcke* was adopted by German scout pilots, and these guidelines were soon used by Allied pilots as well:

Try to secure the upper hand before attacking. If possible, keep the sun behind you.

G   **DOGFIGHT**

Sopwith Camels of 'Naval 8' are locked in a dogfight with Albatros DVs of Jasta 23 in the opening days of 1918, high above the coastline near Calais. 'Naval 8' Squadron was based out of nearby Bray-Dunes aerodrome, and so skirmishes against their neighbours of Jasta 23 were common, and bitter rivalries developed. The German propaganda machine viewed scout pilots as a glamorous commodity to be exploited to raise morale at home; successful scout aces were encouraged to paint their aircraft in distinctive colours, making them easy to recognize by their enemies. Whilst the personalizing of aircraft was all but completely banned by the hierarchy of the RFC, some RNAS squadrons added personal touches to their aircraft, the most famous example being Raymond Collishaw's 'Black Flight', or in some cases bright squadron colours such as the blue and white of 10 Naval Squadron.

The Albatros DV and its DVa development were the last of the Albatros scout family to see service in the war. Richthofen described the DV as 'Obsolete and … ridiculously inferior to the English', thus placing Jasta 23 at a distinct disadvantage when pitted against the Camels of 'Naval 8', one of the best scout aircraft of the entire war.

The dramatic dogfights of the naval scout squadrons of the Western Front would soon pass into history as the RNAS and RFC were amalgamated into the RAF on 1 April 1918. But in only a little over two decades, the pilots, observers and gunners of the Royal Navy would return to the skies of Western Europe as an independent fighting force once more.

The 2F1 Camel replaced one of its two Vickers guns with a Lewis gun on the top wing. Whilst the Vickers was easier to synchronize, the Lewis was lighter and could be swung down on a rail in front of the pilot to change its 97-round magazine.

Always carry through an attack when you have started it.

Fire only at close range and only when your opponent is properly in your sights.

Always keep your eye on your opponent, and never let yourself be deceived by ruses.

In any form of attack it is essential to assail your opponent from behind.

If your opponent dives on you, do not try to evade his onslaught, but fly to meet it.

When over the enemy's lines never forget your own line of retreat.

Attack on principle in groups of four or six. When the fight breaks up into a series of single combats, take care that several do not go for one opponent.

Royal Flying Corps ace Edward 'Mick' Mannock put together his 'Fifteen Rules for Air Fighting', many of which agreed with Boelcke's:

Pilots must dive to attack with zest, and must hold their fire until they get within one hundred yards [91.4m] of their target.

Achieve surprise by approaching from the East.

Utilise the sun's glare and clouds to achieve surprise.

Pilots must keep physically fit by exercise and the moderate use of stimulants.

Pilots must sight their guns and practise as much as possible as targets are normally fleeting.

Pilots must practise spotting machines in the air and recognising them at long range, and every aeroplane is to be treated as an enemy until it is certain it is not.

Pilots must learn where the enemy's blind spots are.

Scouts must be attacked from above and two-seaters from beneath their tails.

Pilots must practise quick turns, as this manoeuvre is more used than any other in a fight.

Pilots must practise judging distances in the air as these are very deceptive.

Decoys must be guarded against – a single enemy is often a decoy – therefore the air above should be searched before attacking.

If the day is sunny, machines should be turned with as little bank as possible, otherwise the sun glistening on the wings will give away their presence at a long range.

Pilots must keep turning in a dog fight and never fly straight except when firing.

Pilots must never, under any circumstances, dive away from an enemy, as he gives his opponent a non-deflection shot – bullets are faster than aeroplanes.

Pilots must keep their eye on their watches during patrols, and on the direction and strength of the wind.

Reginald Alexander John Warneford, VC, wearing a Royal Navy officer's greatcoat as part of his flying gear. Commander R. M. Groves said of Warneford: 'This youngster will either do big things or kill himself.' Warneford was unfortunately killed shortly after receiving his Victoria Cross, when his aircraft suffered structural failure and he, along with his passenger, were flung from their cockpits.

A highly respected pilot and leader, Mannock's rules were also adopted by the RNAS. Flight Lieutenant C. R. Mackenzie of 'Naval 8' also promulgated his own notes, his emphasis being on fighting in formation. As aircraft of the period had no radios with which to communicate with each other and so could only signal via gesticulating from cockpit to cockpit, or waggling wings, the formation flying mentioned above became vital for scout pilots. Aircraft serviceability and pilot availability made it impossible to standardize the size of a formation of scouts, but Mackenzie wrote his rules for a formation of five aircraft. He placed these aircraft in an arrowhead formation, with the flight leader at the head. The leader would fly as slowly as possible, to allow the other aircraft in formation to accelerate and catch up if they drifted away for any reason.

The formation would be as closely spaced as safely possible in order to allow for better communications. Rocking the wings laterally would call for attention, which when accompanied by waving arms or a red Very light would signal enemy aircraft. Rocking the machine in a fore and aft direction would indicate jammed guns, and firing a green Very light warned of technical problems and was a request for an escort back to the lines. As far as possible it was down to the formation leader to deliver signals; if another pilot saw the enemy first, he would break formation and accelerate ahead of the leader to obtain his attention before signalling. Mackenzie also had his own ten rules on attacking hostile aircraft, many of which were similar to Boelcke's and Mannock's. He also warned against the dangers of attacking at too high a speed, where the aircraft was harder to control and the amount of time with which to fire accurately was too short.

By the end of the war, the rules established over the past four years were taught as a standard part of the formalized flying training to scout pilots of both sides. These rules would be just as relevant throughout World War II and into the Korean War, only being made obsolete with the invention of guided air-to-air missiles and engagement distances extending outside of visual range, and even then only in part. The pioneering scout pilots of World War I entered combat with literally nothing to go on, and through trial, error and valour they were able to write the rule book for generations of combat pilots.

MUSEUMS

For both the enthusiast and those with merely a passing interest, the first place to find out more about the early days of naval aviation should be the Fleet Air Arm Museum. Located just outside the perimeter fence of RNAS Yeovilton in Somerset, the Fleet Air Arm Museum boasts the largest collection of British naval aircraft, memorabilia and research material available. At the time of publishing, the museum had recently undergone a large revision to celebrate 100 years of naval aviation, and now houses some of its earliest aircraft in Hall 1.

Available for viewing are replicas of a Sopwith Pup and Short S27, as well as the remains of an original Short Type 184, unfortunately heavily damaged when German bombs hit the Imperial War Museum in 1940. The museum's extensive collection is regularly changing to rotate more aircraft through the display halls. Also at the museum are a replica Sopwith Triplane, Sopwith Camel and Albatros DVa, a composite Sopwith Baby and a smaller-scale

Raymond Collishaw, second from the left, is photographed with his squadron. Collishaw was the RNAS's top-scoring ace, with 60 confirmed kills, many in his black Sopwith Triplane 'Black Maria'. Some historians have credited him with 81 kills unofficially, which would place him ahead of Manfred von Richthofen. Collishaw rose to the rank of air vice-marshal in the RAF during World War II.

H **TACTICS**

The modern definition of the Immelmann turn, whilst devised in World War I, is unlikely to have been devised by Immelmann himself. The contemporary Immelmann turn was a steep climb to a near stall, quickly followed by a sharp rudder turn into a steep dive. The Fokker Eindecker with which Immelmann is synonymous did not have the power to carry out the Immelmann turn depicted at (**1**). More powerful scouts entering service in the second half of the war, however, would not have a problem in being able to pull through a half loop followed by a half roll at the top. This manoeuvre was mainly used for evasion, quickly and efficiently changing height and heading in an attempt to shake off an attacking aircraft.

The manoeuvre shown at (**2**) shows a basic pair tactic known as 'The Sandwich'. Whilst the *Dicta Boelcke* advised pilots to attack in groups of four or six, scout pilots of the RNAS and RFC would often patrol in much smaller groups than those of the German *Jastas*. The small tactical element of the pair was the most flexible formation, not hampered by the constraints of manoeuvring a large, cumbersome formation around the sky. This lesson would be forgotten and relearned several times in several wars throughout the 20th century. Here, an enemy aircraft attacks the pair from the rear. Both scouts turn in to face the attack, the wingman of the pair slotting in behind the enemy aircraft to protect his leader. Tactics such as these were fine in theory, but would often be abandoned in the swirling mêlées of early air combat, especially when communication between aircraft was nigh on impossible.

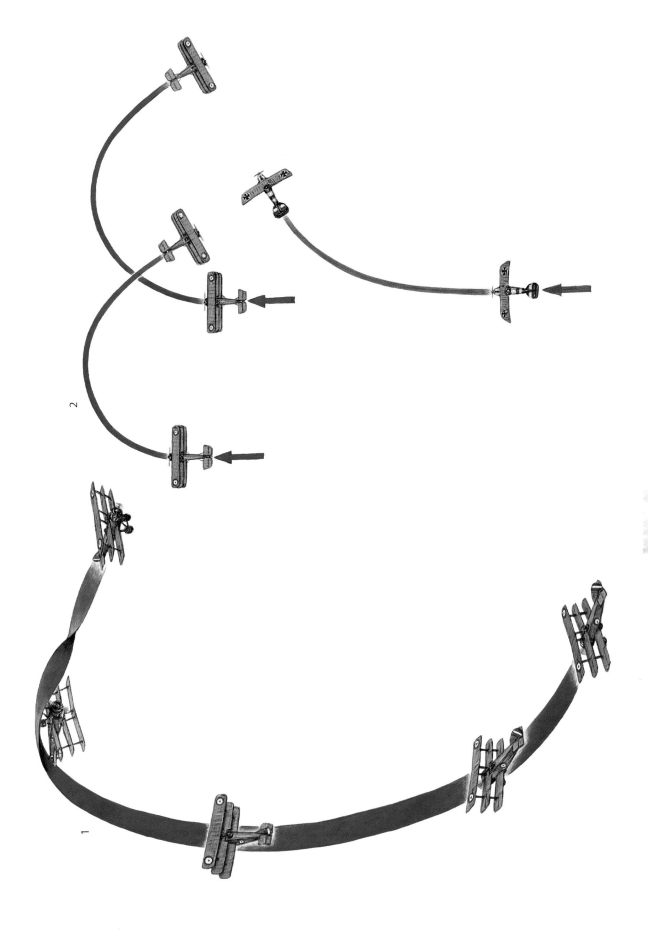

Fokker Dr.I reproduction. The museum also has countless photographs, diaries, uniforms, examples of flying clothing and many other unique items of the period, either on display or in the archives and available for viewing by appointment.

For authenticity in mint condition, the Imperial War Museum, Lambeth is home to one of the world's seven original surviving Sopwith Camels. The Camel is a 2F.1 naval variant, N6812, and was used by Flight Sub-Lieutenant Stuart Culley to shoot down Zeppelin L53. The Imperial War Museum is also an excellent source of information on World War I aviation in general.

However, to see history come alive first hand, there is no finer collection of airworthy historic aircraft of the period in the UK than that of the Shuttleworth Collection, based at Old Warden airfield in Bedfordshire. The collection is available for viewing throughout the year, but is best viewed during the summer months, when the aircraft are flown in spectacular air displays. Shuttleworth is home to no fewer than nine aircraft of World War I; six of these types saw service with the RNAS, and two of these are originals. The four replicas are a privately owned Bristol Scout Type D, Sopwith Triplane, Bristol Boxkite and a Sopwith Camel, under construction at the time of publishing. The original aircraft are an Avro 504K that entered service with the RAF in 1918 and a Sopwith Pup that served aboard HMS *Manxman*. The replica Sopwith Triplane is painted as an aircraft of 'Naval 8' and is powered by an original 130bhp Clerget rotary engine. The staff of the Shuttleworth Collection are themselves experts in their subject matter, keeping history alive now that the last World War I survivors have unfortunately passed away. Helpful and friendly, the men and women who keep these pieces of history airworthy are available to talk to when visiting the collection.

The National Museum of the United States Air Force is also an excellent source of information and houses an interesting collection of aircraft of the period. An Avro 504K, Sopwith Camel and Nieuport 28 are all on display, but the museum also has many other aircraft of World War I used against and alongside those types employed by the RNAS.

A Submarine Scout Zero blimp tethered to HMS *Furious*. The ship was originally designed as a cruiser, armed with two single 18in. gun turrets. The forward turret was removed during construction and replaced with a 49m-long flight deck; the aft turret was removed after trial firings in July 1917 showed the hull could not handle the recoil.

SELECT BIBLIOGRAPHY

Bartlett, C. P. O., *In the Teeth of the Wind*, Leo Cooper: Barnsley, 1994

Bell-Davies, Richard, *Sailor in the Air*, Seaforth Publishing: Barnsley, 2008

Cooksley, Peter G., *The RFC/RNAS Handbook 1914–18*, Sutton Publishing Limited: Stroud, 2000

Cormack, Andrew, *British Air Forces 1914–1918*, Osprey Publishing: Oxford, 2000

Draper, Chris, *The Mad Major*, Air Review Limited: Letchworth, 1962

Finnis, Bill, *The History of the Fleet Air Arm*, Airlife: Shrewsbury, 2000

Franks, Norman, *Sopwith Pup Aces of World War One*, Osprey Publishing: Oxford, 2005

Gibson, Mary, *Warneford, VC*, Fleet Air Arm Museum: Yeovilton, 1979

Hallam, T. D., *The Spider Web*, Arms and Armour Press: London, 1979

Layman, R. D., *The Cuxhaven Raid*, Conway Maritime Press: London, 1985

McCudden, James, *Flying Fury*, Greenhill Books: London, 2000

Rosher, Harold, *In the Royal Naval Air Service – Being the War Letters of the Late Harold Rosher*, Naval and Military Press: Eastbourne, first published 1916

Steel, Nigel and Hart, Peter, *Tumult in the Clouds*, Coronet Books: London, 1997

Thetford, Owen, *British Naval Aircraft Since 1912*, Putnam Aeronautical Books: London, 1991

INDEX

Figures in **bold** refer to illustrations.